D0777191

the mighty voice of
paul
robeson

sing and shout

Susan Goldman Rubin

CALKINS CREEK
AN IMPRINT OF BOYDS MILLS & KANE
New York

For information about permission to reproduce selections from this book,
please contact permissions@bmkbooks.com.

Calkins Creek
An Imprint of Boyds Mills & Kane
calkinscreekbooks.com
Printed in Spain

ISBN: 978-1-62979-857-8 (Hardcover)
ISBN: 978-1-64472-052-3 (eBook)
Library of Congress Control Number: 2019939633

First edition
10 9 8 7 6 5 4 3 2 1

Design by Barbara Grzeslo
The type is set in Dante.

To the memory of Paul Robeson
and the artists and activists who followed

I did not come here to solve anything.
I came here to sing
and for you to sing with me.

Pablo Neruda,
"Let the Rail Splitter Awake"

contents

preface

Paul Robeson was an artist and social activist whose voice could not be ignored. Millions of people responded favorably to him and what he stood for. For me, personally, perhaps his most important gift was his mentoring. The only other voice that carried sway in public thought and opinion in the twentieth century championing the cause of those who were racially and economically oppressed was that of Dr. King. They were the two major forces in guiding activists to a courageous place of resistance against segregation. Any journalist, social commentator, or, in this case, author who chooses to write about Paul Robeson and to tell the story of his courage and the sacrifices he made is a welcomed opportunity. I wholeheartedly suggest that *Sing and Shout: The Mighty Voice of Paul Robeson* be read by all.

Harry Belafonte,
singer, songwriter, activist,
actor, and author

foreword

Activism among young people is not a new phenomenon. From the Civil Rights movement of the 1950s and 60s to the Black Lives Matter movement of today, young people have consistently spoken out.

Paul Robeson was a true Renaissance man, a man who achieved success as a scholar, athlete, lawyer, singer, author, and actor, but he was most famous for channeling those talents as an activist. Robeson used his tremendous voice to rail in the first half of the twentieth century. Robeson epitomized the willingness to sacrifice and do what he felt was right, even if it was unpopular or seen as too radical. A great modern-day example is Colin Kaepernick and his brave stand to take a knee during the national anthem, reminding us that not all people are truly free in America. Kaepernick's unequivocal commitment to activism follows a tradition of athlete-activists like Muhammad Ali, Jackie Robinson, and, of course, Paul Robeson.

This book explores the rich history of who Paul Robeson was and how his legacy remains important today.

It's hard to adequately describe or convey how prominent and effective Paul Robeson was. He remains one of the remarkable scholars, activists, and talents of modern times. On a full scholarship, Robeson studied at Rutgers University in New Brunswick, New Jersey. By the time he graduated from the university, Robeson had received an unprecedented twelve major letters in sports, while also giving a stirring commencement address. Continuing his education, he ultimately earned a law degree from Columbia University Law School. When he tried to pursue a career at a big New York City law firm, he faced countless episodes of racism. Disheartened but undeterred, he turned his talents to acting and singing, where he felt accepted and confident enough to speak up for racial justice. With his amazing gift of languages —he spoke fifteen—Robeson would end up traveling the world, using his fame to break down barriers.

The son of a runaway slave, Robeson encouraged black communities to join together to heal, support, and uplift one another. This notion is relevant today, as black people continue to be targeted, marginalized, and victimized because of the color of their skin. Coalition building is essential to the longevity of the black community. Robeson fought for equitable resources and services that the black community deserved. Even today the black community struggles for racial justice. Young people can model Robeson's efforts to sustain equity and justice in economics and voting rights, systems that have been historically designed to disenfranchise people of color.

Acts of racial injustice are longstanding in our country. Robeson knew this was an ongoing challenge, not one to be solved overnight. He once said, "the answer to injustice is not to silence the critic but to end the injustice." Robeson recognized the importance of speaking out again and again until the injustice ends.

Everyone should commit to examining the ways Paul Robeson used his many talents to be a voice for change. His work for justice is not done. It will not be done until people of color are no longer marginalized or victimized by racial injustice. As you read this book and reflect on Robeson's life and legacy, I challenge you to be more like Robeson—to be an active ally. I challenge you to take a stand against injustice and do something to make a positive difference. We all have the ability to be effective social justice change agents. Moving forward, make it an actionable goal to improve the current conditions of society and do what is right to help make our communities more just and inclusive. Let's honor Paul Robeson's name and speak up and speak out against all forms of injustice so everyone can live a life that is unapologetic, authentic, and free from oppression; where infinite liberation is reached, and justice always prevails. Robeson's legacy is relevant today now more than ever before, so let's do our part to uphold that legacy and be the change we wish to see in the world.

Dr. David E. Jones,
Director of the Paul Robeson
Cultural Center at Rutgers University
in New Brunswick, New Jersey

a note on terms used in this book

This book uses the term "Negro" because Paul Robeson did. He proudly owned his identity. In the foreword to his book *Here I Stand*, the first sentence reads, "I am a Negro." He repeated these words throughout his career, in interviews, speeches, and writing, and referred to himself and his people as Negro. Sometimes he added, "The origin of the Negro is African," for Robeson took immense pride in his African heritage.

Although he identified the spirituals he sang as "Negro spirituals" and "Negro American folk music," he excitedly researched their African origins. His wife, Eslanda Goode Robeson, wrote a biography of him, *Paul Robeson, Negro*, published in 1930. In the early twentieth century, the word "Negro" was preferred as a term of respect. However, this word is not used today. Language for describing race is constantly evolving. Robeson, ahead of his time, used the terms "black" and "Afro-American" interchangeably with "Negro" throughout his life. The terms "black" and "African American" became popularized in the 1960s, '70s, and '80s. This biography reflects the period of history in which Robeson lived. With great respect, I have quoted his words and those of his family and friends.

personal note

In 1954, when I was a student at the High School of Music & Art in New York City, a friend invited me to hear Paul Robeson speak at somebody's apartment. I knew that Robeson was an acclaimed black singer and actor, famous for concerts of spirituals, as well as theater and movie performances. My parents saw him play the role of Othello on Broadway and still talked about it. But when I left the apartment that night, my mother warned, "Don't sign anything."

After hearing Robeson speak passionately about injustices he suffered, I signed the petition that was passed around. It felt good to have my teenage voice counted for what I believed was a righteous cause. Now that I have researched and written a young adult biography of Robeson, I realize more fully what that petition was about, and I'm proud that I added my name. We, the signers, deplored Robeson's "domestic arrest" and championed his right to travel outside the country. He was seeking support from students and liberals, so he could have his passport returned. It had been revoked in August 1950, just as he was about to leave on a concert tour. FBI agents had stormed into the home where he was staying and demanded he turn over his travel document. Robeson, with his lawyer present, would not give it up. In those days of the Cold War and McCarthyism, the FBI targeted Robeson because he spoke out about colonial freedom and the position of black people in the United States.

Robeson, son of an enslaved man, knew that he was being singled out because of his race, and he wanted to call attention to discrimination. The government was attacking him because he delivered speeches about the treatment of black people in America, Africa, and colonial countries. At a hearing before the House Un-American Activities Committee in May, 1955, Robeson said, "I am not being tried for whether I am a communist. I am being tried for fighting for the rights of my people, who are still second-class citizens in this United States of America."

—SGR

Paul Robeson in the 1920s, around the time he gave his first concert of spirituals in New York City

i'm gonna sing and shout

— "By 'n' By"

By 7:30 p.m. on April 19, 1925, crowds gathered outside the Greenwich Village theater in New York City. People clamored for seats in the little theater, which was already sold out. At 8:15, a sign announced: Standing Room Only. Inside, those lucky enough to be seated waited expectantly for what was touted as the "music event of the year."

Backstage, twenty-seven-year-old Paul Robeson stood in the wings "paralyzed with fright." His tuxedo was already soaked with sweat even though performing in public was nothing new to him. He had starred in Eugene O'Neill's plays *All God's Chillun Got Wings* and *The Emperor Jones* in this very theater with the Provincetown Players. In November, he had given a small solo concert in Boston that was well received.

But tonight's concert was different because of the music Robeson and his accompanist Larry Brown were about to perform. Although the theatergoers had been led to expect greatness, would the mostly white audience like the songs? Their program consisted entirely of what were then called "Negro spirituals." Many of the songs told stories from the Old Testament, set in a time when the Jews were captives of the Egyptians. Enslaved black people in America used these stories as a basis to express their religious faith and ease their suffering. Nobody wrote the spirituals. The songs came from people's souls. "It was really their own plight they were describing in words and music," said Robeson. "The liberation theme struck so deep," as in "Go Down, Moses":

17

Paul Robeson (seated on the right) in a scene from Eugene O'Neill's play *All God's Chillun Got Wings*

Go down, Moses, way down in Egypt land
Tell old Pharaoh, Let my people go.

The spirituals were songs passed down orally to give coded directions to enslaved people escaping on the Underground Railroad. Would a white audience in New York City consider these songs worthy of a concert? Would they grasp the true meaning behind the words or just consider the songs to be curious renditions of music heard in black Southern churches of the past? Would they simply boo Robeson off the stage, ending his singing career before it started?

These were the days of Jim Crow segregation. Separate but equal was the law of the land, established by a Supreme Court ruling after a light-skinned black man had dared to sit in a train car reserved for whites. Not only were trains segregated, but also buses, schools, baseball parks, and playgrounds. Public facilities in the South and parts of the Midwest had signs marked "White Only" and "Colored." At a Florida train station, a railing divided the stairs—whites on one side, blacks on the other—so that the soles of their shoes wouldn't touch the same stair.

Even in downtown New York, where Robeson had been performing as an actor, blacks were barred from restaurants and hotels, and forced to sit in balcony seats in theaters, except at "progressive" houses such as those where the Provincetown Players put on shows.

The *New York Amsterdam News*, one of the oldest black newspapers in the country, regularly published editorials and reports about lynchings in states from Virginia and Florida to Texas and New Mexico. In 1925, mobs had killed sixteen black people, including two women. The Ku Klux Klan, a viciously racist organization, had swelled in membership. Chapters were springing up all over the country and were considered legal and respectable. In this type of environment, could Robeson hope to win over an audience?

Some black people criticized the practice of singing spirituals

Lawrence Brown in the 1920s

A self-portrait of Carl Van Vechten,
photographer and music critic, who helped
Robeson and Brown put on their first concert

in public, calling it a reminder of the days of slavery. Others thought the songs should be sung in harmony with a chorus, as was traditional. Brown, a black musician born in the South, had arranged the spirituals in a modern style. Robeson would take the solo parts, and Brown would echo the choral responses—like a "call and response" in church, when a preacher called out and the congregation answered. Robeson said, "Brown guided me to the beauty of our own folk music and the music of all other Peoples so like our own."

The men had first met in London when Robeson was there performing in a play called *Voodoo*. Then they had bumped into each other recently in New York. For fun, they began singing at Robeson's apartment. Robeson's wife Essie, who usually didn't like spirituals because she thought they were "monotonous and uninteresting," was excited. She thought that her husband and Brown were "a perfect combination." With her encouragement, the men teamed up professionally. At parties, they performed the spirituals to the delight of glamorous guests: composer George Gershwin, publisher Alfred Knopf, and dancer Adele Astaire, sister of famous dancer Fred Astaire. One of Robeson's influential white friends, Carl Van Vechten, a patron of black artists, raved about the spirituals and arranged for this public concert.

Robeson and Brown had been practicing for weeks. Robeson said that Brown coached him "as if we were children he was teaching," and added, "we slept like children all week, not to catch a cold." Now, both dressed in evening clothes, they were about to make their debut. Brown tried to hide his nervousness as he strode onstage and sat down at the piano. Robeson, a six-foot-two former athlete, froze. Millia Davenport, the Provincetown Players' costume designer, said, "With all my strength I [pushed him] onto the stage—to make history." The audience greeted the musicians with cheers and applause that lasted three minutes.

The houselights dimmed. Robeson faced Brown and rested a hand on the piano. Then, with a nod, he signaled that he was ready to begin.

In his deep, powerful, bass-baritone voice, Robeson sang "Go Down, Moses":

When Israel was in Egypt land
Let my people go
Oppressed so hard they could not stand,
Let my people go

He delivered the words naturally, with feeling, and let his memory "carry him back to that little church [his father's] where he had heard them sung so often." Later, he explained that he had "unconsciously absorbed the manner of singing spirituals as they should be sung." "By 'n' By," the fourth song in the set, opened with Brown's high tenor leading. Robeson then repeated, in his characteristic low tone, "By 'n' by, I'm gonna lay down this heavy load." The audience clapped wildly after each number. The applause made Robeson and Brown forget to be self-conscious, so they just sang "simply, unaffectedly, and beautifully," recalled Essie.

The next set consisted of secular folk songs: "Scandalize My Name" and the wistful "Li'l Gal." Then Robeson slowly began, "Water Boy, where are you hi-i-din'?" without any piano accompaniment. Avery Robinson, the white Southerner who had transcribed the work song, told Robeson that he sang it exactly as the black chain gang had the first time he had heard it. As Robeson began the joyous "Joshua Fit De Battle Ob Jericho," Brown chimed in, "Oh, yes," and they finished in unison, "And the walls came a tumblin' down."

At the end of the concert, the audience went crazy. After numerous curtain calls, Robeson and Brown sang sixteen encores. Exhausted, they finally ended the evening by having the houselights turned up.

The following day, critics marked the concert as a triumph and enthused over Robeson. Typical of the times, reviewers noted his handsomeness as well as his music. "It will be long before any of us will forget the spectacle of this magnificently built man . . . [and] the soft beauty of his voice." The *New York World* commented, "Paul Robeson's voice is difficult to describe. It is a voice in which deep bells ring." The revered black sociologist, author, and activist W. E. B. Du Bois was in the audience that night. He sent Robeson and Brown a note saying, "May I tell you how much I enjoyed the fine concert last night. It was very beautiful."

Robeson was thrilled with their success. "I couldn't possibly ask for anything more," he told a newspaper reporter. Right away, public demand for concerts increased, and offers of recording contracts came in. Agents competed to represent the duo. Two years later, when Robeson was on his way to perform in Europe, he sent a note to his friend and patron, Van Vechten: "Every time I appear in a strange capital I shall think of that first concert," he wrote, "and your unselfish interest and thank you all over again. Because it was you who made me sing."

a motherless child

— "Sometimes I Feel Like a
Motherless Child"

"The glory of my boyhood years was my father," wrote Paul Robeson.
"I loved him like no one in all the world." When Paul later gave concerts,
he sang spirituals his father might have sung on the plantation, such as
"Many Thousan' Gone":

> *No more auction block for me*
> *No more, no more*
> *No more auction block for me*
> *Many thousan' gone*

His father, William Drew Robeson, was born enslaved in Martin
County, North Carolina. At age fifteen, William escaped and made his
way to Pennsylvania on the Underground Railroad, a network of safe
houses providing shelter to help enslaved people travel north so they
could live free. Working as a farmhand, he earned tuition for Lincoln
University, the first college in America granting degrees to black students.
William took courses in Latin and Greek, and he graduated in 1873 with
honors. Three years later, he earned a degree in sacred theology, and
became a minister.

Paul described his father's speaking voice as the "greatest" he had
ever heard, "a deep, sonorous basso, richly melodic and refined." When
Robeson performed, he would affectionately imitate his father delivering

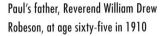
Paul's father, Reverend William Drew Robeson, at age sixty-five in 1910

a sermon in a "voice going down like an organ."

While William was a divinity student at Lincoln, he met and fell in love with Maria Louisa Bustill, a young teacher from Philadelphia. Louisa, as she was called, was a tall, slender woman with a keen mind and remarkable memory. She was also known for her gentle manner and cheerful disposition. Often, she visited her uncle who lived in Lincoln, Pennsylvania. Louisa came from one of Philadelphia's prominent black families. The Bustills descended from freeborn African Americans, and family members had intermarried with English Quakers and people of the Lenni-Lenape Indians who lived in what is now Delaware. One of the Bustills had been a member of the Underground Railroad chain and had helped over a thousand enslaved people gain freedom.

William and Louisa married in 1878, and settled in Princeton, New Jersey. He was appointed pastor of the Witherspoon Street Presbyterian Church. Louisa, like William, was highly intelligent as well as deeply religious, and she helped her husband compose his sermons. They lived in the parsonage a few doors down from the church. There, they raised their children: William Drew, Jr. (called Bill), Reeve, Benjamin (Ben), a

Paul's mother, Maria Louisa Bustill Robeson, 1878, age twenty-five, at the time of her marriage

The house where Paul Robeson was born at 110 Witherspoon Street, Princeton, New Jersey

daughter Marian, and the youngest, Paul Leroy, born April 9, 1898. As the baby of the family, Paul was the favorite, and his siblings doted on him.

When Paul was two years old, his older brother Bill tried to enroll at Princeton University but was turned down. At that time, the beginning of the twentieth century, the town of Princeton was segregated like a Southern Jim Crow town. Black people were not welcome at white shops or restaurants up on Nassau Street. As Paul wrote, "Almost every Negro in Princeton lived off the college and accepted the social status that went with it. We lived for all intents and purposes on a Southern plantation." At the movie theater, they had to sit in the back section. The one black physician in town was refused staff privileges at the Princeton Medical Center and Hospital, so his patients had to go to a hospital in Trenton. The university itself was off-limits to black students. Even the gate at the entrance of the campus "was always locked shut. It was never open—never," recalled a resident of the black Witherspoon Street neighborhood.

Nevertheless, Reverend Robeson went to see Woodrow Wilson, a professor at Princeton and the future president of the university. Wilson was also a governing elder of the Presbyterian Church. Reverend Robeson appealed to Wilson to admit his brilliant son Bill to the college. Wilson angrily declared that Princeton did not accept "colored." This incident may have been the reason Reverend Robeson lost his ministry in 1901.

Other factors played a role as well. The reverend had developed the Witherspoon Street Presbyterian Church as a center of civic and social activity for the black community. Congregants knew him as "the defender of justice," standing firmly for the rights of his race. However, white Presbyterians still controlled the church and forced him out. Initially, they criticized him for not making the church financially independent. Yet an investigation showed that nothing was amiss. Certain white residents of Princeton were said to want the reverend to stop speaking out against lynching and race riots, which he refused to do. Many years later, Reverend Robeson received an apology from the Presbyterian Church for the injustice done to him.

The Robeson family moved from the parsonage to a run-down house around the corner on Green Street. Paul later described it as a "shack" that was "so bad it should have been condemned." His father earned a little money by hauling ashes from white people's fireplaces in a horse-drawn wagon and driving Princeton University students around town. Paul admired his father for never complaining and wrote, "He was still the dignified Reverend Robeson to the community, and no man carried himself with greater pride."

Paul's mother suffered from chronic asthma and cataracts in her eyes that left her nearly blind. She depended on Paul and Ben, who were still living at home, to lead her about the house. A family friend observed that Paul was his mother's "little guide and inseparable" from her.

One morning in January 1904, Reverend Robeson went shopping in Trenton. Paul was at the Witherspoon School for Colored Children down the street from his father's former church. Ben, age eleven, had stayed home to help his mother. Louisa asked Ben to put a piece of new linoleum under the stove. As they tipped the stove, the door flew open. Hot coals fell on Louisa's long dress, and her skirt caught fire. Ben tried to stamp out the flames. He ran out of the house screaming for help. Neighbors passing by rushed inside and found Louisa ablaze. Someone grabbed a bucket of snow to douse the flames. By the time they put out the fire, Louisa was horribly burned. A doctor arrived and gave her medicine to relieve the excruciating pain.

When Paul returned home from school he watched helplessly. A few hours later, she died. Paul was five years old. "I remember her lying in the coffin, and the funeral, and the relatives who came," he wrote. "But it must be that the pain and shock of her death blotted out all other personal recollections."

His mother was buried in the white section of the Princeton Cemetery. The Presbyterian church owned the cemetery and gave

Witherspoon School for Colored Children, 1904. Paul Robeson, age 6, is probably in the front row, second boy to the left of the pole.

The Princeton YMCA football team champions in 1908. The boy in the second row holding the football is Ben Robeson, Paul's older brother.

Reverend Robeson special permission to have her buried there, near where they lived. Her grave is close to the cemetery gate on Witherspoon Street that Paul passed every day as he went to and from school.

"There must have been moments when I felt the sorrows of a motherless child," he wrote. Singing released his deepest feelings. Years later, at his debut concert, Paul sang, "Sometimes I Feel Like a Motherless Child," and tears streamed down his face. A friend who was at the concert said that she "was crying too, and so was half the audience."

a home in that rock

chapter 3

— "I Got a Home in That Rock"

After his mother's death, Paul grew closer to his father despite the fifty-three-year difference in their ages. "During many of his years as a widower I was the only child at home," wrote Paul, "and his devoted care and attention bound us closely together."

In 1907, when Paul was nine, his father moved to the town of Westfield, New Jersey. The reverend changed his religious affiliation to African Methodist Episcopal and built a small church. While he got settled, Paul stayed in Princeton with his relatives from North Carolina who lived in the neighborhood. They took care of him and fed him well. "I remember the cornmeal, greens, yams, and the peanuts and other goodies sent up in bags from down in North Carolina," he wrote.

"I got plenty of mothering," recalled Paul, "not only from Pop and my brothers and sister when they were home, but from the whole of our close-knit community. . . . In a way I was 'adopted' by all these good people." Their houses were filled with "a warmth of song," he remembered. "Hymn-song, and ragtime ballad, gospels and blues, and the healing comfort to be found in the . . . sorrow of the spirituals."

> *Nobody knows the trouble I've seen*
> *Nobody knows my sorrow*

He heard these songs in his father's sermons, which he said were almost like operas. Singing, clapping, and swaying, Paul joined in the rousing call and response,

I got a home in-a-dat rock, don't you see?
I got a home in-a-dat rock, don't you see?

By 1910, Reverend Robeson had established a parish—St. Thomas A.M.E. Zion—in the town of Somerville, New Jersey. Paul was the only child at home, while his brothers and sister went back and forth from school. Bill first attended Lincoln University, then medical school at the University of Pennsylvania. Reeve also attended Lincoln University for a time, but then dropped out, greatly disappointing and angering their father. When Reeve kept getting into trouble with the law, the reverend sent him away so that he wouldn't be a bad influence on Paul. Yet Paul wrote, "I admired this rough older brother and I learned from him a quick militancy against racial insults and abuse." Ben, Paul's favorite brother, attended a prep school in North Carolina, followed by college. Marian, also in North Carolina, stayed with relatives while she studied at the Scotia Seminary for young black women.

In the evening, Robeson's father gave him speeches to memorize and taught him how to use his voice eloquently, insisting on perfect diction. Afterward, they played checkers. The reverend rarely talked about his early years as an enslaved person. However, his father's infrequent tales were vivid and haunted Paul's memory. He marveled at his father's refusal to remain in bondage. Paul knew what slavery and oppression meant to his family. Songs such as "Deep River," a cry for comfort and hope, became part of his repertoire and evoked his father's suffering. Slowly Paul drew out the first word as he sang,

Dee-ee-eep river
My home is over Jordan.

De-ee-eep river, Lord
I want to cross over into campground

In Somerville, Robeson attended James L. Jamison Colored School, then the unsegregated Washington School in Westfield. After graduating at the head of his class, he spent eighth grade in a segregated Somerville school, and again graduated with top grades. "Pop was pleased by that," said Paul. "He was never satisfied with a school mark of 95 when 100 was possible."

Getting straight A's came easily to Paul at Somerville High. The school had only a few black students, but he got along well with his white classmates. One of his best friends throughout high school was Douglas Brown. They both played on the football team, joined the debating team, and belonged to the glee club. Brown said, "When Paul cut loose, the rest of us in the bass section just had to wiggle our mouths."

The Somerville High School baseball team, 1914. Paul, holding a catcher's mitt, sits in the front row, second from the right. A superb athlete, he held varsity letters in football, basketball, baseball, and track when he graduated in 1915.

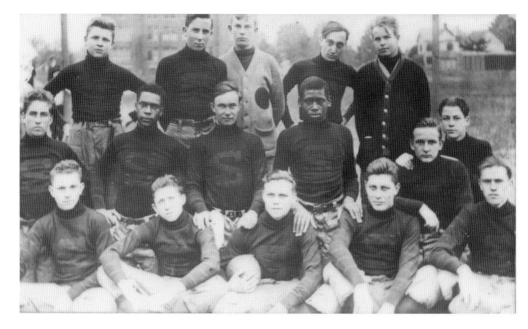

The Somerville High School football team, 1913. Paul is in the second row, fourth from the left.

Paul's music teacher, Miss Elizabeth Vosseler, appreciated his remarkable voice, and urged him to take singing seriously. His older brothers also recognized the quality of his voice. At home, they entertained themselves by harmonizing on popular ballads. Once, when the boys were "chording up on a few tunes" such as "Down by the Old Mill Stream," and "Turkey in the Straw," Paul belted it out. His brother Bill yelled, "Wait a minute, hit that note again, Paul." Paul did. "You can sing!" exclaimed Bill. Paul told him to stop "making stupid jokes." From then on, the family eagerly discussed Paul's "talent," and he sang in his father's church choir as well as in the school chorus.

Sports interested Paul more than music. At six feet tall, he was "good at stopping a man" on the basketball court. But his skill as a football fullback won him the most attention. A teammate said that Paul had such large, strong hands that he could grip a football and throw it like a baseball. His father came to every game, cheering him on. Fellow players on the team thought of the reverend as their good luck charm.

Everyone liked Paul and commented on his "sweetness and modesty." His English teacher, Miss Anna Miller, introduced him to theater. The class presented a skit featuring characters from Shakespeare's plays who meet up at a health resort. Paul took the part of Othello, but he suffered from stage fright. "Nervous and scared, I struggled through the lines," he recalled, ". . . and no one in the world could have convinced me then that I should ever try acting again." Nevertheless, Miss Miller thought he was gifted.

At first, she hesitated to ask him to participate since the purpose of the one-night performance was to raise money for a class trip to Washington, DC. She knew that Paul would not be able to go, because the city was segregated and no hotel would accept a black guest. Still, he wanted to be in the show, "and proved a huge hit with the audience." He even sang that evening. His classmates later recalled that he did not go to Washington with them, but a newspaper article listed his name among the students who made the trip.

Despite Paul's popularity, he "shied away" from what he termed "social affairs." He said, "There was always the feeling that—well, something unpleasant might happen; for the two worlds of white and Negro were nowhere more separate than in social life." His chemistry teacher, Miss Bagg, coaxed him to attend parties and school dances. "When I did so," he wrote, "it was she who was the first to dance with me."

His classmates welcomed him at their homes. A football and basketball teammate said, "All of us were Paul's friends at school as well as after school. . . . Everybody's mother was crazy about him and was always holding him up as an example of what they would like us to be."

"Well, I was a good boy, sure enough," wrote Paul, "but I wasn't *that* good!" He was lazy and overslept in the morning and arrived late at school. In Latin class, he often came unprepared, but when his teacher called on him to translate, he did it perfectly on sight, which made her furious.

In his final semester, when he was seventeen, he wondered what vocation he would choose. "Singer? No, that was just for fun. Dramatics? Not I!" he wrote, looking back. "There was the lingering thought, never too definite, of studying for the ministry; and though my father would have liked that choice, he never pressed it upon me. Perhaps in college I'd come to a decision about a career."

Although he didn't realize it, Paul's natural passion for the "warmth of song" was to shape his life. "I heard my people singing!" he later wrote, "and my soul was filled with their harmonies."

on my journey now

—"On My Journey, Mount Zion"

In Paul's senior year of high school, he heard about a statewide exam for a scholarship to Rutgers College, an all-white school. His father and his brother Bill had both graduated from Lincoln University and wanted Paul to go there too. Even Miss Miller encouraged him to apply to historically black colleges that might present fewer obstacles. "I don't want to have things handed to me," declared Paul. "I don't want it made easy." He took the exam, achieved the highest score in the history of the competition, and won the scholarship.

Paul braced himself for going to one of America's oldest exclusive colleges (today Rutgers, The State University of New Jersey). Of 484 undergraduates, he would be the only black student. The all-male school had accepted only two black men in the past. Could he succeed and live up to the expectations of his father, his family, and his community and be a "Credit to His Race"? Back at Witherspoon School in Princeton, Paul had learned this lesson: "Be a credit to your race. Racism will always be with us. . . . You have to work twice as hard and put twice the effort into what you do."

As Paul was about leave for college, African Americans were debating what was then called "the Negro Problem." How could they restore their image and gain political and economic power after the damages resulting from 400 years of slavery? W. E. B. Du Bois, the first black man to receive a PhD from Harvard University, believed that education was the key. White Americans had to realize that black people had the capacity for higher learning. Yet attitudes about white superiority and vicious lies about black inferiority had been ingrained in the majority of Americans from childhood. "Here was a decisive point in my life," wrote Paul. "Equality might be denied but I *knew* I was not inferior."

When Paul entered Rutgers in 1915, he was not allowed to live with a roommate because of his race. Colleges in the north practiced racism in less-visible ways than horrific lynchings. According to the student directory, he had a single in room 142 of Winants Hall, a dormitory. A couple of his neighbors on the floor were Jewish. Anti-Semitism prevailed at Rutgers at that time, as well as in other parts of the country. Before the outbreak of World War I in Europe in 1914, masses of Jewish immigrants had arrived in the United States. Many had fled from bloody anti-Jewish riots in Russia. The volume of immigrants from Eastern Europe was so high that quotas were established to limit the number of Jews allowed in businesses and schools. Country clubs, hotels, and desirable neighborhoods excluded Jewish people in addition to blacks. Paul later told friends that he felt "an almost unexplainable rapport with Jews."

Winants Hall, the dormitory at Rutgers University where Robeson lived

During his first week on the campus, he experienced hostility from many white students who "stared at him either condescendingly or with open contempt." He sat alone in the cafeteria. Paul hid his anxiety and radiated confidence with a "friendly manner" and an "irresistible smile." Years later, his classmates and professors remembered him as "quietly genial" and an "uncomplaining good fellow who never expressed anger."

Of course, no fraternity would admit Paul to its house. Rutgers' Greek fraternity system shut out African Americans from their brotherhood. Nevertheless, he participated in the "sings" outside the Beta Theta Pi fraternity house, and on the steps of Winants Hall. Wherever he appeared, students would shout "Gopher Dust!" because his performance of that tune was so popular. Everyone recognized him as a "natural singer who loved to share his musical talent."

Right away, he excelled in the classroom. He also loved playing football and wanted to try out for the Rutgers team. Coach George Foster Sanford had seen him play in high school and was impressed. But he did not invite Paul to preseason practice, because veteran players had objected to having a black man on "their" team. Yet Sanford wanted to give Paul a fair chance, so he was allowed to start out with the scrubs. Paul, having grown to almost his full height of six feet, two and a half inches, and weighing 190 pounds, was bigger than the others.

On the first day of scrimmage, the young men on the varsity squad attacked Paul. "They didn't want a Negro on their team," he recalled. "One boy slugged me in the face and smashed my nose, just smashed it. That's been a trouble to me as a singer every day since." Another player fell on him and dislocated Paul's shoulder. Afterward, he limped off the field.

"That night I was a very, very sorry boy," he said. "I didn't know whether I could take any more." He thought about his father's principles. The reverend had reminded Paul of his duty: "I was the representative of a lot of Negro boys who wanted to play football and wanted to go to college, and, as their representative, I had to show that I could take

"Robey of Rutgers" was considered to be the nation's best football player in 1917 and 1918.

Robeson tries for another touchdown in a game between Rutgers and Newport Naval Reserves in 1917.

whatever was handed out." Paul's oldest brother Bill visited him while he recovered from his injuries and gave him a pep talk. "Kid, if you want to quit school, go ahead, but I wouldn't like to think, and our father wouldn't like to think, that our family had a quitter in it."

Paul remained at Rutgers and went back to try out for the football team. This time, one of the players on his own team stomped on his hand. The cleats tore off his fingernails. "That's when I knew rage!" he said. On the next play, he swept out his arms, tackled three men, and grabbed the guy carrying the ball. Paul lifted him up over his head and was about to smash him down to the ground. "I wanted to kill him," he said. But Coach Sanford stopped him at the vital moment and yelled, "Robey, you're on the varsity!" From then on, Robey of Rutgers was gradually accepted and came to be admired by his teammates. Coach Sanford taught him how to calculate his moves and protect himself on the field.

During games, Paul endured racial taunts from the stands. Some southern colleges objected to playing against Rutgers because they had a black man on the team. Once, Coach Sanford had to bench Paul for a game with Washington and Lee University. The visiting Virginians said they wouldn't play if Robeson did. Although some of Robeson's teammates protested out of loyalty to him, the coach bowed to pressure from the administration. The game marked the celebration of Rutgers' 150th anniversary. The administrators were expecting alumni to make gifts to the school, and they didn't want controversy to spoil the festive event. So Paul sat out the game. Later, James D. Carr, a New York lawyer who had been the first African American to graduate from Rutgers, learned of the incident. He wrote a scathing letter to the college criticizing the injustice done to Robeson. Looking back, Paul regretted "acting right" that day and thought he should have refused to ever play another game for the school.

After victories, the Rutgers team enjoyed steak dinners, and between courses, Paul's voice boomed out as he sang college songs like "On the

Banks of the Old Raritan." In December, the town of New Brunswick, home to Rutgers, held a banquet for the team at a hotel. Paul couldn't attend because he was black. Even as he became the team's most honored player, he could not go to celebrations at public restaurants and inns that were segregated. Paul often handled the situation with humor. On one occasion, he kidded a teammate: "I feel sorry for you guys. You got such little helpings out there in the restaurant. In the kitchen they fed me royally!"

Rutgers University football team, star players, 1918. Robeson stands between William Feitner to the right, Alfred Neuschafer to the left, and Joseph Breckley on the far left.

Paul also faced obstacles with the glee club, which never officially accepted him as a member despite his magnificent bass-baritone voice. He sang on campus only, and with the understanding that he would not attend social functions afterward that included white female choruses from other schools. Social mixing of races was condemned because whites feared that the contact would lead to intermarriage and the corruption of their race. Paul was not allowed to travel with the club because Jim Crow laws banned black people from staying in hotels, eating at restaurants, and even trying on shoes and clothes in department stores. Still, he sang at informal gatherings on campus, accompanied by a friend. At proms and military balls, Robeson performed from the balcony above the dance floor so that he wouldn't be mingling with white people.

He used his glee-club appearances and football fame as advertisements for giving private concerts to earn extra money. "I used to hustle around, fix up a concert, and bill myself as a star attraction," he told a reporter. "I would go on the stage, sing a group of songs, orate and flourish for 20 minutes, and then sing again." He also sang at church events. Sometimes, his football teammate, Al Neuschafer, accompanied him on the piano. Once, when Paul performed at a church between the acts of a play, the audience did not want the play to continue. "They preferred to hear more of Paul's singing," recalled Neuschafer.

On Sundays, Paul frequently went back to Somerville, fifteen miles away, to help his father preach. He said, "Before the service was over I would be singing with the rest of them [the congregation]," perhaps "On My Journey, Mount Zion":

> *On my journey now, Mount Zion*
> *My journey now, Mount Zion*
> *I wouldn't take a nothin', Mount Zion*
> *For my journey now, Mount Zion*
> *One day, one day, I was walkin' along*

Well, the elements opened an' de love come down
Mount Zion.

Paul rejoiced in the spirituals and conveyed his delight. His marvelous voice rang out with infectious passion.

For his social life, Paul made friends in the black communities of nearby New Jersey towns. In his sophomore year, when he was eighteen, he delivered a program at the YMCA in Freehold. Paul recited some poetry, gave a dramatic reading, and sang a mixture of popular ballads and spirituals. On that trip, he met a young black woman, Geraldine Neale, and fell in love with her. Geraldine, nicknamed Gerry, was finishing high school and planned to train as a kindergarten teacher. "Everybody knew we were going to be married when we finished school," said Paul. "We were meant for each other."

In those days, dating was referred to as "keeping company." Over the next three years Paul kept company with Gerry while he was at Rutgers and she was at the New Jersey State Normal School at Trenton, studying to be a teacher. With their friends, they held song fests, and Robeson readily agreed to solo. He sang everything from sorrowful songs, such as "Swing Low, Sweet Chariot," to popular love songs. His rendition of "I Love You Truly" sent a tender message to Gerry. It was *their* song. He changed the lyrics of "Gray Days Are Your Gray Eyes" to suit her. "Negro girls have brown eyes," he said. So, for Gerry he sang, "Gray days are your *brown* eyes."

By Paul's junior year, two more black students had enrolled at Rutgers, and they shared a room with him in Winants Hall. Paul maintained such a high grade-point average that he was elected to Phi Beta Kappa, the oldest academic honor society in the United States. As the star of the football team, he gained national recognition. A sportswriter with the *New York World* dubbed him a "football genius," and another described Paul as "the best all-round player on the gridiron this season." Walter Camp, a Yale coach and an authority on football, put Robeson on his

All-American Football Team and called him "a veritable superman."

Yet it was Paul's gifted voice that was to bring him the greatest satisfaction as an adult and draw others to him. Speaking about the little concerts he gave while in college, he said, "These one-man shows were splendid practice."

Robeson proudly shows off his Phi Beta Kappa key.

my heart in pain

— "There's a Man Going Round Takin' Names"

In the spring, at the peak of his triumphs, Paul suffered a terrible blow. His father became ill, and Paul traveled back and forth from Rutgers to Somerville to nurse him. The reverend was sick in bed and knew he couldn't be present when Paul took part in an upcoming oratorical contest at Rutgers. He made Paul promise to compete no matter what happened to him. "I want you to win," the reverend said.

On May 17, 1918, Reverend Robeson died. Paul didn't see how he could go through with the contest as his father's coffin rested in the parsonage parlor. Once again, Paul's older brother Bill, who had returned home from medical school for the funeral, convinced him not to quit. Three days later, Paul kept his word and spoke.

Gerry and supportive friends went to hear him. One of them said, "Paul stood there on the stage, gaunt, sombre, obviously steeped in grief as he talked in that beautiful, moving voice." In his speech, Paul pointed out the few educational opportunities given to black Americans, even though many, like Paul's brother, Ben, were fighting for their country in World War I, which the United States had entered in 1917. Ben was an Army chaplain-in-training at a Kentucky military camp.

That night, at the contest, Paul won first prize, honoring his father's memory. But without his beloved Pop, Paul lost his zest for studying. During his senior year, his grades dropped. Although Paul was at the top of his class, he did not receive highest honors. Nevertheless, his

In 1919, Paul Robeson was one of four men inducted into the Cap and Skull Honor Society, the highest level of tribute for a Rutgers student. The society's motto was "Let us be judged by our actions," and students were chosen on the basis of leadership and deeds.

classmates elected him to Cap and Skull, an honor society.

Coach Sanford mentored him as Paul thought about what he would do as his life's work. His father had wanted him to become a minister, but Paul realized that he lacked the "zeal." They agreed that he would take up law as a profession. With Sanford's encouragement, Paul applied to law school "to make a name for himself and to serve his people." He felt sure that he had "a destiny to fulfill." Yet he wasn't sure what it would be. He only knew that his father had "lovingly prepared him for it" through his sermons and the spirituals.

There's a man going 'round takin' names
There's a man going 'round takin' names
He has taken my father's name
And has left my heart in pain
There's a man going 'round takin' names.

Before graduation, Paul proposed to Gerry. She turned him down. "I was not sure I loved him enough," she said. Her friends were shocked. "Who would ever raise such a question if they could marry Paul Robeson?!" Later, Gerry recalled that, although she loved Paul deeply, she realized even then that "he was a man of destiny and that he would belong to the world, rather than to his family." She wanted a more conventional married life. He refused to accept her answer and kept trying to change her mind. "Gerry—she was just perfect, so sweet," he told a friend, "the one woman in the world for me."

On Commencement Day—June 10, 1919—Robeson, age twenty-one, was asked at the last minute to replace one of the student speakers who had suddenly become ill. Fortunately, Robeson was among those awarded a senior prize for "extempore speaking" (giving a speech without preparation), and he delivered a stirring oratory. "We of this less favored race realize that our future lies chiefly in our own hands," he told the mainly white audience. "And we are struggling . . . to show that knowledge can be obtained under difficulties." Robeson indirectly referred to the Ku Klux Klan, an organization that hated blacks, Catholics, and Jews. The Klan controlled newspapers and public opinion, and membership had recently soared in the North as well as the South. But Paul exhorted the crowd to "catch a new vision," and demonstrate a "fraternal spirit" so that "there will be equal opportunities for all."

He expressed hope for "an era when the richness of the Negro contribution to art and music would win just recognition." Unwittingly, he was forecasting his future as a singer and actor. Already he used his powerful voice to connect with people. Many in the audience later said

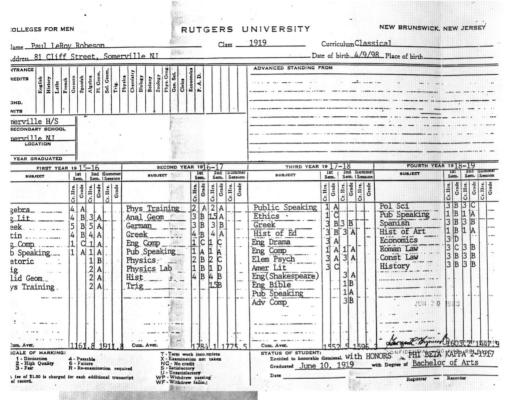

COLLEGES FOR MEN   RUTGERS UNIVERSITY   NEW BRUNSWICK, NEW JERSEY

Name **Paul LeRoy Robeson**   Class **1919**   Curriculum **Classical**

Address **81 Cliff Street, Somerville NJ**   Date of birth **4/9/98**   Place of birth _____

ENTRANCE CREDITS: English, History, French, German, Spanish, Algebra, Pl. Geom., Sol. Geom., Trig., Physics, Chemistry, Biology, Botany, Zoology, Phys. Geog., Gen. Sci., Economics, Civics, P.A.D.

ADVANCED STANDING FROM _____

COND. UNITS

SECONDARY SCHOOL: **Somerville H/S**

LOCATION: **Somerville NJ**

YEAR GRADUATED

FIRST YEAR 1915–16	Cr. Hrs. 1st Sem.	Grade	Cr. Hrs. 2nd Sem.	Grade	Summer Session Grade
Algebra	4	A			
Eng. Lit	4	B	3	A	
Greek	5	B	5	A	
Latin	4	B	4	A	
Eng. Comp.	1	C	1	A	
Pub. Speaking	1	A	1	A	
Rhetoric			1	B	
Trig			2	A	
Solid Geom			2	A	
Phys Training			2	A	

Cum. Aver. 1161.8   1911.8

SECOND YEAR 1916–17	Cr. Hrs. 1st Sem.	Grade	Cr. Hrs. 2nd Sem.	Grade	Summer Session Grade
Phys Training	2	A	2	A	
Anal Geom	3	B	15	A	
German	3	B	3	B	
Greek	4	B	4	A	
Eng Comp	1	C	1	C	
Pub Speaking	1	A	1	A	
Physics	2	B	2	C	
Physics Lab	1	B	1	D	
Hist	4	B	4	B	
Trig			15	B	

Cum. Aver. 1784.1   1775.5

THIRD YEAR 1917–18	Cr. Hrs. 1st Sem.	Grade	Cr. Hrs. 2nd Sem.	Grade	Summer Session Grade
Public Speaking	1	A			
Ethics	1	C			
Greek	3	B	3	B	
Hist of Ed	3	B	3	A	
Eng Drama	3	A			
Eng Comp	1	A	1	A	
Elem Psych	3	A	3	A	
Amer Lit	3	C			
Eng (Shakespeare)			3	A	
Eng Bible			1	B	
Pub Speaking			1	A	
Adv Comp			3	B	

Cum. Aver. 1552.5   1595.3

FOURTH YEAR 1918–19	Cr. Hrs. 1st Sem.	Grade	Cr. Hrs. 2nd Sem.	Grade	Summer Session Grade
Pol Sci	3	B	3	C	
Pub Speaking	1	B	1	A	
Spanish	3	B	3	B	
Hist of Art	1	B	1	A	
Economics	3	D			
Roman Law	3	C	3	B	
Const Law	3	B	3	B	
History	3	B	3	B	

Cum. Aver. 1603.7   1647.9

SCALE OF MARKING:
1 - Distinction
2 - High Quality
3 - Fair
4 - Passable
6 - Failure
R - Re-examination required

T - Term work incomplete
X - Examination not taken
NC - No credit
S - Satisfactory
U - Unsatisfactory
WP - Withdrew passing
WF - Withdrew failing

A fee of $1.00 is charged for each additional transcript of record.

STATUS OF STUDENT:
Entitled to honorable dismissal **with HONORS**   PHI BETA KAPPA 1917
Graduated **June 10, 1919**   with Degree of **Bachelor of Arts**

Date _____

Registrar — Recorder

A transcript of Robeson's grades at Rutgers from 1915 to 1919 shows A's in public speaking for almost every semester until his senior year. His grades slipped after his father's death, yet Robeson graduated with honors.

A portrait of Paul Robeson that appeared in Rutgers' *Scarlet Letter* Yearbook, 1919, with a write-up of his academic achievements and varsity honors that no commencement orator in the history of Rutgers College had received such long applause as Paul did.

That summer, he moved to Harlem, the center of the black community of New York, to prepare for entering New York University. Harlem had previously been a white neighborhood, but it had changed during the start of the Great Migration in the early 1900s, when millions of black people in the rural South began to travel north to find work and escape oppression. Many settled in big cities, such as Chicago and New York, and brought their culture with them. Immigrants from the West Indies arrived too, and they headed for Harlem. In New York, as the population exploded, black people who had been living around Sixty-Third Street relocated uptown along with the newcomers. By 1919, when Robeson arrived, Harlem was the nucleus of black life, and he felt at home there.

He shared an apartment on 135th Street with two of his pals. One of them had a girlfriend, May Chinn, a college student majoring in music. She had a piano in her mother's Harlem apartment and accompanied Paul while he sang. He and May gave small recitals in schools, churches, and private homes to earn money for tuition. But she told Paul that "the cultured, well-educated Negro" asked them *not* to sing spirituals for audiences that included white people. He deferred to her, and they presented lyrical songs such as "Danny Boy," an Irish melody, which later became one of Paul's concert favorites:

> *Oh, Danny boy, the pipes, the pipes are calling*
> *From glen to glen, and down the mountain side.*

Paul didn't know it yet, but he was really preparing for his profession as a performing artist.

we are climbing higher and higher

—"Jacob's Ladder"

Robeson hated New York University Law School. The students in his morning section were "noisy and childish." And it was a long ride from his Harlem apartment. In February 1920, Robeson transferred to Columbia Law School, just a few blocks from where he lived. He was registered in the class of 1923. He had promised his Pop that he would get a law degree, and he thought that law would give him a secure profession. Yet years later, he said, "I really didn't know what I wanted to be and I had no idea what my future would be." Perhaps he would teach constitutional law after graduation.

To earn money for tuition, Robeson juggled part-time jobs. He worked as a Red Cap at Grand Central Terminal in midtown Manhattan. Red Caps helped train passengers by heaving and carrying heavy loads of luggage to and from trains. The men were all African Americans, and hundreds of them graduated from college thanks to their earnings at Grand Central. Robeson's brother Bill had been a Red Cap to pay his way through medical school.

Robeson also sorted mail at the post office. On weekday nights, he coached the football team at Rutgers with his friend, Coach Sanford, and he helped Sanford's son with Latin lessons. He tutored other students at Columbia and performed at small concerts.

With May Chinn as his accompanist, Robeson kept developing his repertoire. She was willing to do modernized versions of spirituals, but she didn't want to perform original spirituals that middle-class black people might find crude. Robeson worked on "Deep River" and "Go Down, Moses" by himself.

As a duo, they appeared at church fundraisers and Columbia Law School social events. They also performed at meetings of the NAACP (National Association for the Advancement of Colored People), formed in 1909 by activists in New York. The group, established to protest violence against African Americans and fight for their civil rights, periodically flew a flag from its Fifth Avenue office window reading "A Man Was Lynched Yesterday." Daily bulletins reported that white mobs brutally tortured and murdered black people that they suspected of stealing hogs, poisoning mules, or insulting a white person. Someone was hanged or burned alive every four days. Events like Robeson and Chinn's concert raised money to support the goals of the NAACP, particularly an anti-lynching campaign. Years later, when Robeson developed his political voice, he became chairman of the American Crusade to End Lynching.

At Rutgers, Robeson had never been able to join a fraternity. Now at Columbia Law School, he was initiated into the Nu Chapter of Alpha Phi Alpha, the first black fraternity that was founded at Cornell University in 1906. Black fraternities had been formed to house and protect black college students on primarily white campuses. Although Robeson no longer lived on campus, and felt completely comfortable at Columbia among his white classmates, he enjoyed good times at the Alpha Phi Alpha house in Harlem.

For more fun, he joined the choir at St. Philip's Episcopal Church and teamed up with his housemate (May Chinn's boyfriend) to sing at amateur vaudeville shows. They "charmed the crowd with their songs." Milton Rettenberg, a classmate at Columbia, had studied music. He organized a quartet with Robeson singing bass, and they harmonized at school functions. Robeson "was deep into his music," recalled another student, William O. Douglas, who later became a U.S. Supreme Court Justice. As Robeson spent more time singing than studying, his grades dropped to C's.

Football also diverted him. Classmates noticed that he missed school on Friday afternoons and Saturday mornings. "Then we discovered the reason," said a law student. "Every weekend Robey was away playing football for a team in Ohio." Robeson traveled by train to the Midwest to play professional football as an additional way of making money. In 1920, pro football was a new sport. Robeson, twice an All-American at Rutgers, was one of the stars of the first season of organized pro football. He had to show up for practice on Saturday and then play on Sunday in order to get paid. His friend Milton Rettenberg loaned him lecture notes so that he could catch up on classes he had missed.

During one game, Robeson suffered a serious injury to his thigh and was rushed to New York Presbyterian Hospital for emergency surgery. The injury left a hole in his thigh like a "great cavern." After the difficult operation, Robeson was in great pain and remained hospitalized for weeks. An assistant surgeon thought of a way to distract him. He introduced Robeson to Eslanda Cardozo Goode. Everyone called her Essie. She worked as a pathology technician in the lab, and was a smart, assertive, extremely efficient young black woman. And she was beautiful.

Essie's version of the story differs. She said she met Robeson when he had just arrived in New York. "Paul was making his way down Seventh Avenue [in Harlem] one glorious summer afternoon in 1919 with a pretty girl on his arm," Essie wrote in her unpublished memoir. "He was greeting friends and admirers along the way with his wide engaging smile." Essie knew the girl with Robeson and stopped to chat so that she could meet the handsome stranger. "He was often to be seen on the corner of One Hundred and Thirty-Fifth or One Hundred and Thirty-Seventh Street, the centre of a group," wrote Essie. "He had a gorgeous bass voice, and could always be counted upon to carry the low voice part in harmonisations when 'the fellows' got together at parties, or even on street corners, where they might be chatting and suddenly burst into song."

A portrait of Eslanda as a young woman in the 1920s

"When she [Essie] saw him she knew right away she wanted him," remembered a friend.

Essie couldn't stop thinking about "Harlem's darling" and dreamed up ways to casually bump into him. At the Gingham Dance, an annual springtime event, she wore a frilly white dress, thinking he might be there. Sure enough he was, and when she won the award as best-dressed woman at the dance, Robeson handed her the prize of ten dollars in gold coins.

They both attended summer school at Columbia University. Essie planned to go to medical school and was taking pre-med courses. She and Robeson began having dinner together at the YWCA cafeteria and going to parties. Soon they were dating. Later, she admitted that she carried out "a campaign to win Paul." She took an interest in his law classes as well as his singing and love of sports. Essie recognized his potential. She "had made up her mind she was going to make something of him."

That summer, Robeson became involved with a group of black students who produced plays at the Harlem YWCA. Since Robeson lived next door, the actors and the director "dragged him in whenever he passed." They begged him to take the lead in *Simon the Cyrenian*, a play about the black man who helps Jesus carry the cross to the crucifixion. Essie encouraged him to try acting in the play. Finally, Robeson accepted the part. Looking back, he said, "How I happened to do that thing is one of those accidents that make me believe it is luck the way things come about for me." Members of the Greenwich Village Provincetown Players attended one of the three performances and were impressed with his acting.

While Robeson continued with his law studies, he and Essie fell in love and talked about marriage. Yet he hesitated. He really wasn't ready to support a wife. Besides, their families might disapprove. Essie's mother, known as Ma Goode, was a descendant of black enslaved people and wealthy Sephardic Jews. She had an olive complexion like Essie and thought that Robeson's skin was "far too dark." Because of her lineage, Ma Goode felt superior to other people, blacks as well as most whites. Ma Goode's father, Francis Lewis Cardozo, had served as secretary of state and state treasurer in South Carolina. Ma Goode married John Goode, a lawyer. However, when Essie was four, John passed away, so she raised her children alone and supported them by building a beauty care business. A leader in the suffrage movement, and a champion for the rights of black women in America, Ma Goode delivered talks throughout Harlem on "The New Negro Woman." Essie regarded her as a role model, but she didn't agree with her mother about Robeson. In Ma Goode's opinion, he "lacked the ambition and drive required for big-time success."

Robeson's brother Ben had his doubts about Essie. He felt she was too ambitious and that her ways were "aristocratic." Ben thought she was not the right woman for his brother and expressed his concerns in a letter.

Nevertheless, on the morning of August 17, 1921, Robeson knocked on the door of Essie's apartment. "He suggested . . . that they go out and get married that day," she recalled. They took the streetcar up to Greenwich, Connecticut, to elope, but they were told they would have to wait five days for a marriage license. On the way back to New York, they passed Port Chester, and Robeson noticed a "Town Clerk" sign. They hopped off the streetcar, dashed into the office, and were married fifteen minutes later. Robeson was twenty-three, and Essie was twenty-five.

A photo of Robeson and Essie taken in London after they were married

At first, they kept their marriage a secret, especially from their families, who disapproved of their courtship. Robeson felt people might think him irresponsible for marrying before he finished law school and started earning a living. He went back to rooming with his friend, and Essie continued sharing a studio apartment with her friend. By December, they felt ready to announce their wedding at the annual conventions of Robeson's fraternity and Essie's sorority, Delta Sigma Theta Sorority for Negro women. She had joined the sorority when she was a student at the University of Illinois. Delta Sigma Theta was dedicated to public service, and Essie actively participated in the New York chapter.

After the holidays, the Robesons moved into a large front room on the top floor of an old brownstone on 138th Street. Their room overlooked ginkgo trees on the quiet, residential street. Essie's mother was "unsupportive," and Ben and Robeson's sister Marian withheld their blessings.

Robeson was disappointed, but he and Essie carried on with their busy lives. Robeson divided his time among law school, football, and occasional singing engagements at Columbia dinners. Essie worked at Presbyterian Hospital as a pathologist–chemist, and made cross sections of tissues taken from patients in the operating room, for viewing under a microscope. She felt she could support them both on her monthly salary if she had to, but this arrangement embarrassed him as a man and provider.

In 1922, the director of *Simon the Cyrenian*, the show that Robeson had performed in at the YWCA, offered him the lead in a play called *Taboo*. The story, set on a Louisiana plantation in the days of slavery, told of a wandering minstrel who brings about rain during a drought because of his voodoo powers. Robeson didn't want to do it, because he needed to focus on his law studies. Essie encouraged him to take the part, and he finally agreed. "I knew little of what I was doing," he said, "but I was urged to go ahead and try."

Taboo opened at the Sam H. Harris Theater in New York in April and closed after four performances. Critics panned the play but praised Robeson's "stage presence" and his "rich, mellow" voice. Alexander Woollcott, the famed drama critic of the *New York Times*, was so fascinated by Robeson's terrible performance that he invited him to his apartment for a chat. Woollcott was known for his biting remarks and advised Robeson "that he belonged almost anywhere but on a stage." Years later he described Robeson in more positive terms: "I never in my life saw anyone so quietly sure, by some inner knowledge, that he was going somewhere."

The dean of Columbia Law School noticed the play reviews. Carrying some newspapers under his arm, he stopped Robeson at school and said, "What have you been doing?" Robeson worried and said to himself, "Well, I guess this is it," meaning the end of his law career. But the dean said, "I read some nice things about you—they say you're a very fine actor." Robeson hadn't seen the papers yet and asked to see the dean's. He read the reviews and realized, "I—well—I was fairly famous."

As he prepared for his second-year law exams, and passed them, he kept thinking about theater. Essie took him to plays, and they discussed the performances and studied the reviews. She said, "It never occurred to him that acting is a serious profession."

A show called *Shuffle Along*, a song and dance revue, was a smash hit on Broadway. It was the first entirely black production—with black producers, writers, composers, and cast—that was a success with racially diverse audiences. The musical comedy had opened at the Belasco Theater in May 1921, where for the first time in New York, outside of Harlem, black people sat in the orchestra instead of being restricted to the balcony. The star of the sensational revue was Florence Mills, a beautiful dancer and singer, just two years older than Robeson.

Skits in the revue featured characters based on stereotypes from minstrel shows, which involved an entertainer who darkened his face with burnt cork and portrayed a character named Jim Crow. The name became a derogatory term for a black man. Although *Shuffle Along*

The original cover of sheet music for *Shuffle Along*, including the hit tune "I'm Just Wild About Harry"

followed the minstrel tradition of comedians in blackface, the terrific new jazz score with hit tunes helped make it popular.

Some of the numbers in *Shuffle Along* were performed by a quartet called the Four Harmony Kings, led by Harold Browning, a friend of Robeson's. On a Saturday night in May, 1922, Browning ran into Robeson on a street corner in Harlem and told him that the bass singer in the quartet had unexpectedly left. Unless they could find a replacement, the Four Harmony Kings would have to drop out of the show. Robeson said, "Brother, you're looking at your bass right here!" Browning

Carl Van Vechten photographed Noble Sissle in 1951.

Lyricist Noble Sissle surrounded
by *Shuffle Along* cast members

seemed skeptical, but he took Robeson home to hear him sing. "He was astonished" at the beauty of Robeson's voice, and his range.

Robeson struggled through rehearsal the next day and appeared in the musical that night. Sporting a straw hat and swinging a cane, he followed the other three in the group onto the stage. Stooping through a narrow doorway to the stage without losing his hat, he tripped over a board and stumbled. Essie, sitting in the audience, "closed her eyes in horror." She was sure he had knocked the other three down. But when she opened her eyes, the Four Harmony Kings were smiling and singing. Eubie Blake, the composer and conductor, said, "That boy will bear watching. Anybody who can nearly fall like that and come up with a million-dollar smile has got *some* personality!" Robeson stayed in *Shuffle Along* for a month until the regular bass returned.

At the end of June, the playwright of *Taboo* asked him to recreate his part for a London production. He would be playing opposite Mrs. Patrick Campbell, one of England's leading actresses. Essie wanted him to do it. She had "set her mind and heart" on pushing Robeson into exploring his gifts as a singer and actor for a full-time career. "He didn't want to be an actor," she wrote, "but how high could he go in his [law] profession? This was America and he was a Negro; therefore he wouldn't get far. If he put his foot on the bottom rung of the ladder of the theater, he could climb to the top."

Robeson had enjoyed performing in *Shuffle Along*. A rumor spread that the musical might open in London, and he hoped he might resume his role as a Harmony King. Although he intended to finish law school, the courses bored him. He decided to skip summer law studies and return to school in the fall. In July 1922, Robeson sailed to England to perform in *Taboo*.

We are climbing higher and higher
We are climbing higher and higher.

chapter 7

england's green and pleasant land

— "Jerusalem"

In early July 1922, Robeson, age twenty-four, arrived in Southampton and said, "I had never seen any land so beautiful—green and companionable." He continued, "The people were so kind. . . . I sensed none of the prejudice I had left." In most of America, Jim Crow laws prevailed, and people were segregated on trains and streetcars, in taxis, at gas stations, and in waiting rooms. A handshake could happen between a black person and a white person only if the white person offered to shake hands, which they often didn't.

When Robeson had played pro football in Akron, Ohio, shortly before going to England, the crowds had booed him. He and Fritz Pollard, an All-American black halfback from Brown University, had not been able to get a hotel room or eat in a restaurant. After one game in Green Bay, Wisconsin, where nearly all the policemen were members of the Ku Klux Klan, they were called out of a dining room and told, "We don't allow colored people to eat in our hotel."

In England Robeson received a "friendly welcome" and was treated with courtesy and respect. He was regarded as a "gentleman and a scholar." "My background at Rutgers and my interest in academic studies were given much more weight than such matters are given in America," he recalled. "I found in London a congenial and stimulating intellectual atmosphere in which I felt at home."

Essie had remained in New York, supposedly to continue her job at the pathology lab in the hospital. She hadn't told Robeson that she needed surgery to remove adhesions from an old appendectomy. Essie was sure that if Robeson knew about the operation he would want to stay with her and would miss his opportunity.

After seeing him off at the pier, Essie wrote twenty-one letters to him, asked one of his friends at Columbia to mail them to Paul at regular intervals, and checked herself into New York Presbyterian Hospital.

Robeson began rehearsals with Mrs. Patrick Campbell. Mrs. Pat, as she was called, had renamed the play, changing *Taboo* to *Voodoo*. She not only starred in the show, but also directed it and rewrote sections of the script. Without knowing that Essie was hospitalized, Robeson sent her cheerful reports. "The play is shaping up fine," he wrote. They planned to try out *Voodoo* in the provinces, English counties outside of greater London, and also in Scotland, to prepare for a London production in August.

Robeson in costume for *Voodoo* during the 1922 British tour

63

On July 17, *Voodoo* opened in Blackpool, a seaside resort. The audience hurled oranges at the actors, who ran offstage. The play received poor reviews and Robeson began to worry. "To be truthful, things are none too rosy," he wrote to Essie. "Mrs. Campbell doesn't know her lines too well. But I guess we'll hit." Still, Robeson considered his options. "I think that if this does not turn out as well as I expected, I'd better head right back and get down to law," he wrote. "Of course, if the play goes, I'll stay; but if not, I think I'd better come back."

The next stop on the tour was Edinburgh, Scotland. Actors on tour couldn't afford regular hotels so they stayed with working-class people who took in roomers. Many young actors resented these "digs," which were located in factory neighborhoods. Not Robeson. He enjoyed living with "labouring folk" and appreciated their "warmth and friendliness." His lifelong love of British working-class people and their songs began on this trip.

Voodoo received a better reception in Edinburgh. The audience was enthusiastic, mainly because of Robeson. During a scene as a wandering minstrel, Robeson was supposed to fall asleep and start whistling as he lapsed into a dream. Since he couldn't whistle, he hummed. Mrs. Pat, standing in the wings, whispered, "Sing it louder, sing it louder." Robeson spontaneously sang "Go Down, Moses" followed by another spiritual. "I was merely singing songs I had learned in church," he said, "and I was staggered to read the criticisms and find I was famous!"

"The audiences loved 'Old Black Joe,' thinking it was a Negro spiritual," he said. However, the wistful song had been composed by Stephen Foster in the nineteenth century. From then on, whenever things didn't go right in a performance, Mrs. Pat told Robeson to sing. And he did.

By the time they performed in Glasgow, the play had quickly "turned into an unaccompanied concert—with some dramatic action," he recalled. To Essie, he wrote, "It is the consensus of opinion that the most enjoyable feature of the show is my singing. Mrs. Campbell is very unselfish. She's always saying when we take our bows at the final curtain: . . . 'it's your show, not mine.' And she says: 'Sing a lot and long—more, more.'"

Mrs. Campbell told Robeson that she thought he was a "real artist" and suggested that he would make "a marvelous Othello." He bought copies of Shakespeare's plays to study. He also began thinking seriously about staying in London after *Voodoo* opened there, to try his luck as an actor.

In his letters to Essie, Robeson urged her to join him. He told her how much he loved and missed her. "So anxious for you to see me and criticize," he wrote. "Know you can help me." He discussed choices for their future and asked for her advice. "I don't want to send for you and then be out of work," he wrote.

Before going down to Plymouth, the last stop on the tour, Robeson returned to London. Black communities in the city had been growing since the end of World War I, with students arriving from Africa and the Caribbean to continue their education. "London was the center of the British Empire," wrote Robeson, "and it was there that I 'discovered' Africa. That discovery . . . has influenced my life ever since."

Robeson stayed at the home of John C. Payne, a friend from Harlem who welcomed black visitors, especially musicians and performers. Payne had come to London to sing baritone in a quartet that performed spirituals and popular songs. He decided to live there permanently to escape the racism he had encountered in America.

At Payne's "flat," Robeson met another American guest, the pianist Lawrence Brown, who had recently completed a European tour accompanying the celebrated black tenor Roland Hayes. Brown was born and raised in Jacksonville, Florida. His grandfather had been enslaved. Like Robeson, Brown had lost his mother at an early age. As a child, he had witnessed the horror of lynchings and vowed never to return to racist America. Yet he valued and honored his heritage and

Lawrence B. Brown in the early 1920s, around the time he met Paul Robeson. They soon became musical partners.

wanted to preserve every detail of Negro music. When Robeson met him, Brown had published the first of his arrangements of well-known spirituals such as "Steal Away," and was working on a second volume.

Steal away, steal away, steal away to Jesus
Steal away, steal away home
I ain't got long to stay here

Robeson was deeply impressed by Brown's serious research and his creative interest in African American folk music. He said of Brown, "It was this musician who clarified my instinctive feeling that the simple, beautiful songs of my childhood, heard every Sunday in church and every day at home and in the community . . . should become important concert material."

One night, "just for fun" at a party, Robeson sang with Brown at the piano. "He had the most magnificent natural voice," recalled Brown. "I knew at once that it was possible for him to become a great singer, but I had no idea then that we would ever work together." After a few days, Robeson left for Plymouth. "Cheerio, old chap," said Brown, and promised to look Robeson up if he ever went back to the States.

Robeson returned to *Voodoo*, but things weren't going well. Mrs. Pat kept forgetting her lines and improvising. She was known to be high-strung and unpredictable, and she delighted in making stinging remarks to the actors. Now, she turned on Robeson, and rather than encourage him, as before, she instead became nasty. His success and good reviews had aroused her jealousy. When critics praised him as the "dominating personality in 'Voodoo,'" she became angry and began losing interest in the show.

Robeson doubted that a London production would happen and thought about what he should do. He wrote to Essie, asking her opinion: "You'll know what to do. . . . You always know." But her letters seemed indifferent. Puzzled, he wondered why she never responded to his questions directly. Finally, in August, he sent her a cable: "All my questions unanswered. Worried. Is anything wrong. All love, Paul."

By then, Essie had been in the hospital for a month. Complications had set in after her surgery and she had come down with phlebitis, inflammation of a vein. She sent Robeson a cable and told him the truth. When he received the news, he was "taken absolutely off-guard." "I cried and cried as tho my heart would break," he wrote to Essie. "I couldn't pull myself together." He wanted to return to New York immediately, but she told him to stay, thinking she might get well enough to join him.

Just then, *Voodoo* closed abruptly in Plymouth. There would be no London production. Robeson booked passage and sailed to New York. As soon as he docked, he rushed to the hospital. With his loving care, Essie quickly improved and was soon able to go home.

But the experience of living and working in England, and being treated with respect, had been a revelation. Robeson realized that the world offered him new possibilities as an artist and as a man. He was discovering the power of his magnificent voice.

get on board

— "Get on Board, Little Children"

At twenty-four, Robeson completed his courses at Columbia Law School. In February 1923, he received his law degree, but his chances of finding a job were slim. There were only 106 black lawyers in New York, and those few found it difficult to build practices. Racism discouraged black men from even entering the profession because they knew they would have to face all-white juries and white judges. Most black men who wanted to be professionals became doctors, like Robeson's brother Bill, or dentists. Robeson hesitated to apply for a position with a law firm. "His heart was not in law," recalled a Columbia classmate. "He felt he was meant to be something quite different," Alexander Woollcott observed when he had talked with Robeson the previous year.

The Columbia Law School class of 1923. Paul Robeson is wearing a bow tie and stands near the left end of the fourth row.

Essie worried. She was the kind of woman who made things happen. Robeson's inaction irritated her. "He idled away month after month, waiting for something that would interest him to come along," she said.

"Something will turn up," said Robeson. He needed to feel a sense of purpose, a calling, or what his brother Ben called "inner revelation."

During this period, Robeson often visited the office of his friend William Patterson. Patterson's Harlem firm was one of the only black law offices in the city. "When important cases came up whites certainly would not consider a black lawyer," remembered Patterson. "Even a black man in need of a lawyer . . . thought twice about hiring a fellow black. Most blacks could not afford lawyer's fees . . . they preferred a white attorney, who . . . stood a better chance of winning the case."

Patterson suggested that Robeson consider going into city politics, but Robeson wasn't interested. The man who would later become an outspoken activist didn't care about politics then. "I don't even think he voted," said Patterson. In June, a Rutgers alumnus and trustee invited Robeson to work as a clerk in his all-white firm on Wall Street. "This was an extremely important offer," wrote Essie. The firm specialized in big estate cases and was then involved in handling the will of Jay Gould, a millionaire railroad executive and one of the richest men in America before his death. The heirs to his fortune battled over their inheritance. Essie claimed that Robeson prepared the brief, a written summary of points submitted to the court. "No one could work more intensively, more brilliantly, more consistently than Paul when he stumbled into something which interested him," she wrote.

From the start, however, the law office staff treated Robeson with hostility. He was the only black person there. One day, he buzzed for a stenographer to take down a memorandum for him. She refused, saying, "I never take dictation from—," ending with a racial slur, and stormed out.

Robeson discussed the degrading insult with his boss, who sympathized. He admired Robeson's ability yet told him frankly that his prospects were limited. The firm's white clients would probably never let him try a case before a judge. Instead, he generously offered Robeson the chance to open and head a branch of the firm in Harlem. Robeson thanked him but said no. "If I'm going to face this all my life, I might as well get out," he decided. He had encountered and endured prejudice before, but this time he said he would never enter "any profession where the highest prizes were from the start denied to me."

Robeson had applied for the New York State bar exam but changed his mind and didn't take it. He had been indifferent to law studies all along. One of his artist friends said that Robeson was "temperamentally unsuited to the profession." The pull of the arts was stronger. Having experienced success as a performer in *Shuffle Along* in New York, then in *Voodoo* in England, Robeson wanted more of that informal creative life. "More and more, acting had begun to make sense to him."

"Something will turn up," he repeated. As months went by, he spent time reading at the 135th Street Branch of the New York Public Library (now part of the Schomburg Center for Research in Black Culture). The library was an artistic center for African Americans. Evenings at the library, he attended lectures given by black leaders such as Walter White, an officer of the NAACP, and W. E. B. Du Bois, the noted scholar and activist. Du Bois had founded *Crisis* magazine, which published editorials expressing anger over racial injustice. Besides reading and listening to speakers, Robeson enjoyed singing in the library's basement auditorium, home to the Krigwa Players Little Negro Theatre.

For a few weeks, he performed in the chorus of *Plantation Revue*, a song and dance show at the Plantation Club in Harlem. Florence Mills, who had shot to fame in *Shuffle Along*, starred in the musical. Robeson was thrilled to appear with her again and said, "How proud I was when she gave me a nod and a smile of recognition." Robeson and the other two chorus members wore flashy, striped overalls and large straw hats stereotypical of black minstrels. Although he detested the costume, he liked singing "Li'l Gal," one of the numbers in the show, and after work,

Robeson, on the left, in the chorus of Plantation Revue, 1923. The show had a set that looked like a southern plantation with a stereotyped minstral character, Aunt Jemima flipping pancakes.

he left the club humming the tune. The show closed after thirty-three performances, but the charming song later became part of his concert repertoire.

In the fall of 1923, Robeson sent a note to playwright Eugene O'Neill. O'Neill had recently presented *The Emperor Jones* with the Provincetown Players in Greenwich Village. The show starred Charles Gilpin, then the most famous black actor in America, and Robeson asked O'Neill if there were any other parts for black actors. O'Neill suggested that they stay in touch.

A month later, the director of the Provincetown Players invited Robeson to audition for the lead in O'Neill's new play *All God's Chillun Got Wings*. The director's assistant heard Robeson read. "All I remember

Robeson and Mary Blair in the Provincetown Players
production of *All God's Chillun Got Wings*, 1924

Robeson in the Provincetown Players production
of *The Emperor Jones*, 1924

is the audition—and this marvelous, incredible voice," she said. "I can tell you, he [Robeson] was a most impressive personality." Robeson landed the role, and the play was scheduled to open in spring 1924.

The play told the story of Jim Harris, an aspiring black law student who marries Ella Downey, a young white woman and his childhood playmate. But Ella's deep-seated prejudice destroys her love for Jim and she goes mad. As Robeson waited for rehearsals to begin, he sang at public events. He could easily sing any song in several different keys. At parties, he spontaneously sang popular ballads, often without an accompanist. However, it seemed as though no one wanted to hear spirituals, the music that mattered most to him. But when he performed for the NAACP, "he liked to sing the familiar songs from his childhood. Spirituals were the core of the program."

> The gospel train's a comin'
> I hear it just at hand
> Hear de car wheels rumblin'
> And rollin' thro de land
> Oh, get on board, de little children
> Get on board, little children
> There's room for many a more

In late March, Robeson briefly played the lead role of the preacher in the Lafayette Players' revival of a play titled *Roseanne*. The all-black company performed for a week in Harlem's Lafayette Theater, and then in Philadelphia. Reviewers praised the actors more than the play. "Robeson is a strapping man with a voice that rolls out of him like a vibrant tide," wrote a black critic. "It would be 'extremely interesting' to see what he could do with *Emperor Jones* or the frustrated young negro [sic] in *All God's Chillun Got Wings*."

Rehearsals for *All God's Chillun* were postponed again when the leading lady, Mary Blair, became ill. Meanwhile, hostile reaction to the play's theme of an interracial marriage flared up in the press. "Riots Feared from Drama," proclaimed headlines in the New York *American*. The uproar intensified when a rehearsal photo showed Mary, as Ella, kneeling at Robeson's feet and kissing his hand. At that time, laws prohibiting interracial marriage were common in many states. Hate groups in New York demanded that the mayor stop the play from opening or there would be race riots.

The Provincetown Players grew fearful as rehearsals began. They received hate mail. Bomb scares terrified cast and crew. The Long Island branch of the Ku Klux Klan threatened violence against Robeson and O'Neill. O'Neill stood his ground and refused to shut down the play. Finally, the mayor forced him to divert public attention away from *Chillun* and put on a one-week revival of *The Emperor Jones*, starring Robeson.

Now Robeson had two major roles to learn at the same time, and only two weeks to prepare for *Jones*. Could he do it? Would his brilliant intellect see him through? He had had no dramatic training. No coach. He had to rely on instinct.

In *Chillun*, he played a lawyer, a familiar profession. *Emperor Jones* was entirely different. The plot centered on a railroad porter, Brutus Jones, who gets into a fight during a craps game and kills a man. He winds up in a prison chain gang, escapes, and becomes a self-proclaimed emperor of a small island in the Caribbean, where he is eventually killed by his rebellious subjects. Robeson knew what it was like to work as a porter, having been a Red Cap at Grand Central. Was that enough to bring his character to life?

He studied the script in earnest. Essie recalled, "For days and nights eating, sleeping, walking, talking, he would be learning his lines; he even dreamed them." Essie helped him. They ran lines when they were in bed, when they got up, and when they ate. Her mother, Ma Goode, who was temporarily living with them, said that even *she* had memorized half the script.

Essie sat in on rehearsals while the director, Jimmy Light, told Robeson to "feel his way" in the part. "I can't tell you what to do," Light said to Robeson, "but I can help you find what's best for you."

"Let yourself go, Paul," he'd call out from the auditorium. "You look as though you're afraid to move."

"I am," Robeson answered. "I'm so big I feel if I take a few steps I'll be off this tiny stage."

"Then just take two steps," said Light, "but make them fit you."

The first dress rehearsal on May 4th didn't go well. Robeson was "stiff, nervous," Essie noted in her diary. The next day, though, he was "easy and natural." The play opened the following night. Essie attended with her mother and Robeson's sister Marian, who had become a teacher in Philadelphia. "Paul was superb," wrote Essie. By the final curtain, "applause and stomping and whistling, [were] deafening." Robeson received five curtain calls. Critics went wild about his performance. "Robeson held his audience enthralled," reported the *New York Telegram*. "He has a powerful voice that fairly booms."

That evening, the celebrated actor Charles Gilpin was in the audience. After seeing the show, he quarreled with O'Neill backstage. Gilpin had originated the role of Brutus Jones and felt it belonged to him, although he credited Robeson with being a "hard worker" who had "studied intensively." Privately, O'Neill agreed that Gilpin had been better in the part. Still, he decided to use Robeson in any revival of the play and in a production planned for London, because Gilpin kept changing the wording of the script.

Robeson took one day off, then went back into rehearsals for *Chillun* while performing in *Jones* at night. The opening of *Chillun* was set for May 15th. Hours before the curtain was due to rise, the mayor's office announced that it was denying the Provincetown's license to employ child actors for the first scene. Although they gave no reason, the scene portrayed black and white children playing together. On opening night, police surrounded the theater in case protesters mobbed the building. The mayor issued an order to block traffic on the street. O'Neill's steel-worker friends guarded the dressing rooms and theater lobby. The cast and audience were tense. One critic carried a revolver for protection. When the houselights dimmed, the director stepped out and announced that because of the mayor's ban, the opening scene would not be performed. Instead, he read it aloud, and then the performance began.

Robeson later said, "When I went on to the stage, I half expected to hear shots from the stalls." The show went smoothly, though, without any upsets. Essie said, "The audience seemed gripped, moved," and "[was] generous with applause." Critics disliked the play but complimented Robeson. The *New York World* hailed Robeson as "a genius" and "a great actor."

The black press reacted less favorably. The *Afro-American*, the oldest family-owned African American newspaper in the United States, described *Chillun* as "a hard play to sit through. To see a big, respectable and cultured character as the slave of a slim, depraved and silly white woman isn't the kind of enjoyment calculated to make up a good evening's entertainment." The NAACP complained that the theme of *Chillun* stirred up sentiment against integration because it dramatized the disastrous results of an interracial marriage. "The Ku Klux Klan would pay to have just such a play as this put on," wrote the reviewer.

Despite the controversy, the show ran for one hundred performances, playing alternate weeks with *The Emperor Jones*. When *Chillun* finally closed on October 10, 1924, Robeson wondered what he would do next. For the year of 1924, he had earned a total salary of only $1,782.15 ($23,000 in 2018 dollars). Should he return to the law? Many friends urged him to resume that career and enter Harlem politics.

Robeson felt convinced that he had found part of his calling as an actor. "I would have more opportunity on the stage to benefit my race," he said. "In the law I could never reach the peak; I could never be a Supreme Court judge; on the stage there was only the sky to hold me back."

the walls came a tumblin' down

— "Joshua Fit De Battle
Ob Jericho"

Robeson's success with the Provincetown Players attracted the attention of artists, activists, and even a movie producer. Oscar Micheaux, America's first black feature filmmaker had his own company, and he asked Robeson to star in *Body and Soul*. Micheaux wanted to make uplifting black dramas in urban settings. In 1924, movies were silent, so Robeson couldn't use his superb voice. But he accepted the part Micheaux offered because it gave him a big salary of one hundred dollars a week ($1395 in today's dollars) for three weeks of shooting.

In the movie, Robeson played the dual role of an evil convict posing as a preacher, and his sincere, virtuous twin brother. Some scenes involved his playing both parts, so he had to switch personalities within minutes. Micheaux, a novelist turned producer, wrote, directed, and distributed his movies. He made "race films" intended for black audiences, and *Body and Soul* played only in theaters attended by blacks. Robeson disliked the melodramatic film and never spoke about it, but Essie was pleased with his earnings, a total of three hundred dollars. She had given up her job at the lab and now managed his career.

Once again, Robeson waited for a good project to come along. He said, "I realized even then that the number of roles I might ever be able to act were so few, and so far between, that I might starve to death no matter what the critics said about me!" Movie studios cast black actors as servants: maids, cooks, butlers, and bellboys. And black male characters were portrayed as lazy, stupid nitwits. Actor Lincoln Perry, known as Stepin Fetchit, earned a fortune playing a shuffling simpleton. Robeson despised these degrading roles.

He turned down an offer to appear in *Lulu Belle*, a play about Harlem street life. Essie urged him to take it, but Robeson thought the black stereotypes were beneath him. The shady characters of the melodrama did not represent the Harlem people he knew and respected.

By now, Robeson was a well-known actor in New York. He and Essie were invited to parties, and they mingled with an interracial group of leading figures in the arts and politics. Whenever he had the opportunity, at parties or friends' houses or even on street corners, he sang. It was singing he loved most. One of his friends said, "Paul's voice was like something from another world—sweet—if you can talk about a man's voice being sweet."

Sculptor Antonio Salemme had met Robeson during the rehearsal period of *The Emperor Jones*. After seeing the play, he asked Robeson to pose in his Greenwich Village studio. Salemme said of Robeson, "He had this presence, which was both dignified and disarming at the same time."

Robeson posing for sculptor Antonio Salemme in his Greenwich Village studio in the 1920s. Over a period of two years, Salemme created many sculptures of Robeson, including a larger-than-life nude statue entitled "Negro Spiritual."

For a nude sculpture, Salemme placed Robeson in a standing position and said, "Just think of 'Deep River.'" Robeson would raise his arms and start to sing. His voice was so beautiful that Salemme didn't know whether to work on his sculpture or just listen. Robeson said to Salemme, "I enjoy singing to you. You seem to get more than the voice, the music, the words; you know what I'm thinking, what I mean, what I feel when I sing."

While he posed, Robeson tried out songs he was learning and experimented with various vocal effects. He discussed his concerns and goals. "If I can teach my audiences who know almost nothing about the Negro, to know him through my songs and through my roles," he said, "then I will feel that I am an artist, and that I am using my art for myself, for my race, for the world." Salemme titled the bronze statue of Robeson "Negro Spiritual."

The two visited galleries so that Robeson could learn more about visual arts. Sometimes, when Robeson arrived for a sitting, he seemed depressed. One time, Salemme asked him what was wrong, and Robeson said, "I went to see an old friend of mine uptown, and I had to take the freight elevator." Racial slights hurt Robeson, but he held his anger.

During the run of *The Emperor Jones*, Walter White and his wife attended a performance. White was blond, fair-skinned, *and* black. His great-grandmother had been enslaved, and she had borne children fathered by her master, William Henry Harrison, the future president. White used his unusual appearance to pass as white so he could investigate gruesome lynchings and race riots in the South. Back in the North, he gave speeches and lobbied to initiate legislation that would end the hideous crimes.

After seeing Robeson in *The Emperor Jones*, White and his wife planned to have dinner with Robeson and Essie. "We wanted supper and a place to talk," recalled White. "Place after place was suggested and discarded" because of discrimination. They couldn't find a good restaurant where they would be waited on. The two couples decided not to spoil the mood of the evening with a nasty confrontation, but instead rode a bus uptown to Harlem so they could be served without "fear of insult."

White and his wife invited Robeson and Essie to interracial gatherings in their home in Harlem. White was one of the leaders of the Harlem Renaissance, a flowering of cultural activity that showcased black writers, visual artists, musicians, and performers. New York was the hub for theater and publishing, and Harlem, attracted artists and writers. A new appreciation had developed for the contributions to America from black men and women. Robeson expressed the spirit of the Harlem Renaissance when he said: "It is through art we are going to come into our own." Artistic achievement, rather than political action, he believed, would advance racial justice.

Poet Langston Hughes said, "The 1920s were the years of Manhattan's black Renaissance. It began with *Shuffle Along* . . . a honey of a show." Because of music in theaters and nightclubs, and serious plays such as *The Emperor Jones*, "white people began to come to Harlem in droves," wrote Hughes. "It was a period when, at almost every Harlem upper-crust dance or party, one would be introduced to various distinguished white celebrities there as guests."

At a party hosted by White, Robeson met Carl Van Vechten and his wife. Van Vechten was a white writer and photographer who passionately supported black cultural figures. He helped Langston Hughes publish his first collection of poetry with his own publisher, Alfred A. Knopf. Van Vechten wrote pieces in mainstream magazines like *Vanity Fair* to promote the work of black artists.

Robeson and Essie attended another party at Van Vechten's elegant apartment two weeks later. The gifted circle of guests included composer George Gershwin and publisher Alfred Knopf. This time, Robeson sang. Van Vechten wrote to a friend that seeing Robeson "singing spirituals is really a thrilling experience."

Occasionally, Robeson sang at a few small concerts and private parties.

Taxis lined up in front of Harlem's famed Cotton Club in the 1920s, to drop off and pick up passengers who had come to hear Duke Ellington's band. During the years of the Harlem Renaissance, people flocked to Harlem to visit the jazz clubs.

A card from the Cotton Club that was saved and treasured. The entertainers and staff pictured on the card were African American. However, the Cotton Club catered to white patrons only. Black people could work there but were not admitted as guests.

THE FAMOUS
COTTON·CLUB
THE ARISTOCRAT OF HARLEM
LENOX AVE. COR 142nd STREET
RESERVATIONS SUGGESTED
PHONE: BRADHURST 7767.

One evening in March 1925, he bumped into Larry Brown, the musician he had met in London. Brown had returned to America to see his dying father in Florida. After the funeral, Brown traveled to Harlem to stay with friends. He dropped off his luggage and went out for a walk. "There, standing on the corner of 135th and 7th Avenue—alone—in front of the bank, was Paul Robeson." Robeson invited Brown to go to Greenwich Village with him to visit his friend, Jimmy Light, the director of the Provincetown Players. "He [Robeson] said we might play some songs," recounted Brown. That night, at Light's apartment, Robeson sang two of the spirituals that Brown had arranged: "Swing Low, Sweet Chariot," and "Every Time I Feel the Spirit." Brown accompanied Robeson on the piano, and joined in as "the second voice."

"It was completely spontaneous," remembered Brown.

The spirituals came from "the most humble of our people," Robeson said, and had "abiding beauty."

Light was enthralled. "Why don't you fellows give a concert?" he suggested. With Essie, they went back to Light's apartment and "threshed out the concert idea." Robeson and Brown would split their earnings fifty–fifty, and each would give Essie ten percent as their agent.

From then on, Robeson and Brown sang spirituals at Van Vechten's glamorous gatherings. Essie noted that Van Vechten "begged for more and more songs." He offered to help them arrange a public concert and wrote letters to influential friends to publicize the event. "We all promoted Paul, his talent was so obvious," said one of the Provincetown Players. This group gave Robeson and Brown use of their Greenwich Village Theater free of charge to hold the concert, set for April 19, 1925. The musicians had only three weeks to prepare. "We chose what we felt were the most beautiful of the spirituals," said Brown.

The concert marked the first time that a black soloist, rather than a choral group, presented a program of "all-Negro music" at a recital for a racially mixed audience. In the late nineteenth century, the Fisk Jubilee

Singers had introduced spirituals and secular songs in concerts to raise money for Fisk University in Nashville, Tennessee. By the early 1900s, though, many members of the group had dropped out, leaving barely enough of them to continue performing.

Robeson and Brown worried about how *their* songs would be received. Would New Yorkers understand the emotions expressed in the lyrics? "They were both very nervous," wrote Essie in her diary the night of the concert. "When the boys appeared, there was thunderous applause, lasting three minutes. Then they sang."

The program contained four sections, beginning with "Go Down, Moses." The words came from the Old Testament. Enslaved people had taken the biblical texts that related to their own experiences:

> *When Israel was in Egypt land*
> *Let my people go*
> *Oppressed so hard they could not stand*
> *Let my people go.*

At the end of the song, the roar of enthusiastic applause startled Robeson and Brown so much that they forgot about their personal worries and just sang spontaneously.

Next came "I Don't Feel No Ways Tired":

> *For I hope to shout glory*
> *When dis' worl' is on fire*
> *Chillen, O glory Hallelujah!*

Robeson had sung these spirituals at church every Sunday. Men and women in the congregation had rocked their bodies to the powerful rhythms. New Yorkers responded too, swaying in their seats.

The second part of the program consisted of folk and dialect songs including "Water Boy" and "Li'l Gal." The dialect songs contained

African American ways of speaking and spelling words that differed from standard English, and they had been performed in minstrel shows. Robeson had sung "Li'l Gal" at the Plantation Club in Harlem and had always liked it. Now he was bringing the tune to the concert stage, softening and lowering his voice to interpret the wistful love song:

> *I's a sighin' for you honey*
> *And I never knows no rest*
> *Li'l gal, li'l gal, li'l gal, li'l gal.*

Robeson changed the mood as he performed spirituals that Brown had arranged, such as "Steal Away" and "Sometimes I Feel Like a Motherless Child." Robeson had said, "If I can recreate for an audience the great sadness of the Negro slave in 'Sometimes I Feel Like a Motherless Child' . . . then I shall increase their knowledge and understanding of my people."

And he did. Men and women wiped away tears. Essie said, "After each number, the applause was deafening."

The duo ended the program with "I've Got a Home in-a-dat Rock," and the rousing "Joshua Fit De Battle Ob Jericho." The enraptured audience shouted and stamped. "The boys got curtain call after call," said Essie. Robeson's spirituals brought down the house, just as Joshua's army had crumbled the walls of Jericho with trumpets and shouts. He was astonished by the response to his music. "I simply couldn't understand it," he said. "I didn't sing these spirituals in any tradition, because I didn't even know any tradition. I knew the songs from the time I was a child and they were mostly songs sung in unison by a lot of people. I just sang them as I felt their meaning."

ol' man river

— "Ol' Man River"

Before setting out on his first concert tour, Robeson traveled to England for a production of *The Emperor Jones*. He and Essie arrived in London in August 1925. She rented a "nice cozy place" on two upper floors of a three-story-house. They loved staying in Chelsea, a neighborhood of painters, poets, and playwrights, with no racial barriers. The Robesons found England "warm and friendly and unprejudiced."

Robeson "felt even more at home in London than he had in America," wrote Essie. They ate in fine restaurants "without fear of the discrimination which all Negroes encounter in America." At the theater, they could sit in any section. In New York, they were restricted to the balcony.

The Emperor Jones opened on September 10, 1925, at the Ambassadors Theatre in London's West End, a dazzling area packed with theaters, restaurants, shops, art galleries, and museums. Critics praised Robeson, but they disliked the play, which closed after a short, five-week run.

However, Robeson's fame spread. Critics hailed his "wonderful voice" and "astonishing emotional powers." Reporters interviewed him repeatedly. The British Broadcasting Corporation invited him to sing over the radio. Robeson was elated: "I am thrilled at the prospect of talking and singing to—how many is it?—ten million British listeners. . . .

The delight of it almost scares me." In an interview, he revealed his plan to pursue a concert career. "You can easily exhaust the dramatic roles that a negro can choose from," he said, but "there is no end to the songs one can sing if one has the voice."

Reporters treated him with respect, calling him "Mr. Robeson," a courtesy he rarely received back home. They posed questions about his life in the United States as a black man. He opened up and enjoyed talking about his past, his experiences growing up, the lessons he learned from his father. A journalist asked if the slavery stories his father told him had left him bitter. Robeson replied, "Why no! . . . Those bad times are over. What we have got to do is to go forward . . . I realize that art can bridge the gulf between the white and black races." His concert in New York with Brown had proved this, for he had connected emotionally with the audience through the spirituals. Now his voice reached a wider audience through radio broadcasts and recordings.

Before returning to America, he and Essie vacationed in Paris. At the famed Shakespeare and Company bookstore, a gathering place for aspiring writers, they met Ernest Hemingway, James Joyce, and Gertrude Stein. The owner of the store invited the Robesons to a Sunday afternoon salon, and Paul charmed everyone by singing spirituals and Negro workmen's songs. From Paris, Robeson and Essie traveled to the Riviera in the South of France. The warm sun soothed his chronic sinusitis, a problem for him ever since a football teammate at Rutgers had smashed his nose.

In December, they sailed home to prepare for a thirteen-city concert tour with Larry Brown. The first stops in Pittsburgh, Philadelphia, and Detroit were successful. But in February 1926, when they arrived in Chicago for a performance, the auditorium was only half full. Something had gone wrong and the program had not been advertised. Still, Robeson "made up his mind to give these few people as fine a recital as he possibly could," recalled Essie.

Robeson studies a score, as Brown accompanies him on the piano. They spent hours rehearsing new songs and arrangements for concerts.

At the end of the program, critics and audience members cried out for encores. The *Chicago Herald-Examiner* wrote, "I have just heard the finest of all Negro voices and one of the most beautiful in the world . . . Long before he had finished his first group of spirituals, Robeson had moved his listeners to tears, to laughter, and to shouted demands for repetition."

In Boston, Robeson had caught one of his frequent bad colds and needed to rest. When they tried to check into a modest hotel, they were turned away because they were black. Housing laws in Boston discriminated against black people and forced them to live in segregated neighborhoods. Essie snubbed the laws and took Robeson and Brown to the Copley Plaza, one of the fanciest hotels in town, where they were received "with every courtesy." Robeson stayed in bed on the day of the performance. His throat was sore and raw. That night, in the dressing room at Symphony Hall, he said to Brown, "I feel awful. Well, boy, here's where I let you down. I haven't any voice at all. My throat's tied up in a knot, and I can't possibly sing a note." He offered to go out and apologize to the audience for disappointing them.

Brown stayed calm and said, "I think you ought to try one or two songs, anyway." Essie agreed. "Paul was so frightened that he walked on the stage in a trance," she recalled. "He never sang so badly in his life." Somehow, Robeson got through the whole concert, and the audience sympathized. But he was "so shocked at his performance that he declared he would never sing again."

Robeson, Essie, and Brown returned to New York "greatly discouraged." Robeson lost confidence. Essie recommended that he work with a voice teacher. She said, "There must be some way to sing well, at least fairly well, over a cold" and "nervousness." Essie found a coach and said to her, "I've married the most beautiful Voice I've ever heard, and I want you to help me with it." Robeson studied with the coach and learned how to relax his throat so that he wouldn't feel tired. He also consulted with a doctor who treated him for inflammation of his nose and throat. Within a month, his condition greatly improved, and in gratitude, he sang for the doctor's family.

By spring 1926, he accepted the lead in a play titled *Black Boy*, the story of a black prizefighter. Rehearsals began in August. During out-of-town tryouts, police gathered in anticipation of violence when Robeson appeared onstage dressed in skimpy boxing shorts, and romanced a white woman as part of the story. In Wilmington, Delaware, half the audience walked out. Nevertheless, celebrities turned out for the opening night on October 6 at the Comedy Theatre in New York. Reviews were mixed. Several critics expressed gratitude that the script called for Robeson to sing twice, giving them relief from the author's words. Alexander Woollcott wrote, "when Robeson sings . . . the play is just pushed to one side."

Black Boy closed after thirty-seven performances. Robeson, disappointed, announced that he was through with theater. Few parts were open to a black actor. "I can make good with my singing," he said.

Composer Jerome Kern saw the play in a tryout run and had a deep emotional response to Robeson. Kern and his collaborator, lyricist Oscar Hammerstein II, were developing a new musical based on Edna Ferber's best seller *Show Boat*. The story told of a floating theater on the Mississippi in the nineteenth century. The show, like the novel, explored racial prejudice by introducing a subplot concerning a mixed-race character, and it would feature an interracial cast. As Kern sat in the audience watching *Black Boy*, the music of the main song came to him. "The melody of OL' MAN RIVER was conceived immediately after my first hearing Paul Robeson's speaking voice," he later wrote in a letter. "Robeson's organ-like tones are entitled to no small share of 'that thing called inspiration.'"

After composing the song, Kern visited Robeson in his Harlem apartment and played it for him on the piano while Robeson sang from a rough draft. They went downtown to sing it for Oscar Hammerstein II, who wrote the lyrics. Kern and Hammerstein dedicated the song to Robeson. They intended to have him sing "Ol' Man River" three times in the show, playing the lead of Joe, a good-natured but lazy stevedore on the riverboat. Kern even planned to feature a "Robeson recital" in the second act.

Kern and Hammerstein negotiated a contract with producer Florenz Ziegfeld, dubbed Broadway's greatest showman, who produced lavish revues called Follies. No African Americans performed in the shows, and no black people were allowed in the audience. The one exception was the famous comedian Bert Williams, who Ziegfeld hired to star in the Follies from 1910 to 1919.

Putting a deal together with Ziegfeld took time, but the Robesons needed income right away. Essie hurriedly assembled a brochure to drum up billings for more concerts, so that her husband could earn a living. For a one-night performance in a large city, Robeson's standard fee was $1,250 ($12,500 in today's dollars). In January and February 1927, Robeson and Brown returned to the concert circuit and performed in Kansas City, Missouri. The group organizing the concert couldn't afford his usual fee, so he agreed to sing for $750 ($10,230 in 2018 dollars).

Brown accompanying Robeson in a concert of spirituals around the time of their New York debut

In 1913, Kansas City had officially adopted Jim Crow laws. African Americans had separate neighborhoods and public schools. But when Robeson and Brown came to Kansas City, they broke down racial barriers. According to local custom, white people usually sat in a reserved separate section at a concert. Roy Wilkins, then a black reporter and later the head of the NAACP, purposely booked the concert in a large church attended by white people. Wilkins announced that seating would not be segregated. "White folks decided they couldn't stay away," he wrote, and the concert was a huge success.

When Robeson returned to New York, Essie told him that she was pregnant. She was ecstatic. He had "mixed feelings." First of all, he worried about Essie. "You know you're not strong enough," he said. "I'll never forgive you if you ruin what is left of your health for a baby." But she was determined. "I'll take a chance," she noted. He was still struggling to build his career. With a baby coming, he needed work to support his family. So he and Brown arranged to do a series of concerts in Europe, starting in Paris.

Robeson had still not been hired to star in *Show Boat*, although the composers and producer envisioned him in the role of Joe. Essie encouraged him to take the part if it were offered, but he resisted. Robeson had never wanted to perform in a Broadway musical. The segregated seating in Broadway theaters disgusted him, and he saw the personality of Joe as a stereotype. He also objected to the opening lyrics, which included the hated "n-word." The spirituals that he and Brown performed were his "art." In an interview, he said, "I feel that the music of my race is the happiest medium of expression for what dramatic and vocal skill I possess. . . . Negro music is more and more taking its place with the music of the world."

By the time Ziegfeld offered him the part of Joe, in October 1927, Robeson was on his way to France. Reluctantly, he left Essie behind in New York, since she was due to deliver the baby in a few weeks. From the ship, he wrote to her: "So hard to leave you, sweet. . . . But you'll come to me soon, and I'll work hard and do you proud." On November 2, 1927, Essie gave birth to a son, Paul Robeson Junior. "He was an exact replica of his father," she recalled joyously. "The likeness was so startling." When Robeson heard the news, he wrote to Essie, "How can that boy have a crooked nose; he didn't play football. Or was it the delivery. He sounds grand. Won't I be glad to see him. . . . Take good care of him and tell him about papa."

The delivery had been difficult, and Essie developed serious complications that kept her bedridden. As soon as Robeson found out about her illness, he left Brown in the middle of the concert tour and sailed home. Onboard the steamship, he wrote to Essie: "Just you wait and see how I shall treasure you and the boy who is part of us." By coincidence, he reached New York the day before *Show Boat* opened on Broadway. A classically trained singer who had also performed spirituals in concerts was the composers' second choice for the lead, and he starred as Joe. The musical was a smash hit, as Essie had predicted.

But weeks later, producer Florenz Ziegfeld invited Robeson to play the role of Joe in London. The production of *Show Boat* was scheduled to open on May 3, 1928, at the Royal Drury Lane Theatre. This time, Robeson accepted the part. In April, he sailed to England and celebrated his thirtieth birthday aboard ship. Essie planned to join him and leave the baby in New York with her mother, Grandma Goode. Robeson sent a letter to Larry Brown saying he hoped they could resume giving recitals after the play opened.

Robeson arrived at the Royal Drury Lane Theatre during a rehearsal. Kern, seated at the piano on the stage, rushed over and hugged him. "My God, Paul, it's marvelous to see you!" he exclaimed. He led Robeson to the piano and had him sing "Ol' Man River" right then. A member of the cast said, "Paul just walked up and put his arm on top of the piano, and this beautiful voice, this organ of a voice, came out as he sang 'Ol' Man River.' And we were all in tears."

the little wheel runs by faith

— "Ezekiel Saw the Wheel"

Robeson found the rehearsals of *Show Boat* "so trying" that afterward he would go back to the hotel and stay in bed. He couldn't wait till Essie was healthy enough to join him in London and take care of him. He admitted, "I'm still rather a 'baby.'"

Show Boat opened at the Royal Drury Lane Theatre on May 3, 1928. Critics complained about the length of the musical—three and a half hours! But they praised Robeson, saying he "remained superb" throughout the long evening. The *Sunday Times* suggested that the producers cut a half hour of the "inept and clumsy" show and replace it with Robeson singing spirituals.

Robeson with cast members from the London production of *Show Boat*, 1928

Many black people objected to Robeson's character Joe as another "'good-natured, lolling darkey' stereotype," reported a correspondent for the *New York Amsterdam News*. Others resented the lyrics of "Ol' Man River," just as he had, and criticized him for singing a racial slur. Two weeks after the opening, Robeson made a recording of the song in London and removed the racial slur with Hammerstein's permission. Robeson knew that his character, Joe, suffered because he came from a heritage of enslavement, as he did. The people who had attended his father's church in Princeton were a "servant class," he wrote. He remembered that his father had hauled ashes like a garbage man when he had lost his ministry in Princeton. When Robeson sang, he emphasized the lines dealing with oppression:

> *You and me, we sweat and strain*
> *Body all aching and racked with pain*

The song was so popular that the producers of *Show Boat* had the words printed on a cloth curtain that was lowered between scenes so that the audience could see as well as hear them. Sometimes the show was stopped by demands for Robeson to sing another chorus. "People went out of their minds about him," recalled an actor. A chorus girl said, "He tied that show up in a knot." People crowded outside his dressing room waiting for a chance to see him, talk to him, and get an autograph.

One evening in June, Queen Mary and King George V unexpectedly attended a performance. Robeson became so frightened and nervous that he started singing "Ol' Man River" off-key. He couldn't regain his voice and became very upset. "Afterward he cried like a child," recalled the chorus girl. However, the queen seemed sympathetic and returned for another performance when Robeson was in better form.

Show Boat and Robeson's records were huge hits and moneymakers. Essie was delighted to hear the news when she arrived in London. Her mother was taking care of the baby in a vacation house in Oak Bluffs on Martha's Vineyard in Massachusetts. Oak Bluffs was a historically African-American resort for the elite. Robeson and Essie had vacationed there with friends the summer before Paul Jr. was born.

Eslanda (Essie) and Paul Robeson, Jr., age two, on Hampstead Heath in London

My parents devoted almost their entire attention to each other." Paul Jr. would later write, "Grandma Goode was to be my primary caregiver for most of my childhood." Soon, Essie brought her mother and the baby to England, and they all lived in an elegant mansion on Hampstead Heath, a fashionable suburb, while Robeson performed in town.

Larry Brown had returned to London from Paris. He and Robeson gave a few concerts on Sunday afternoons at the Drury Lane, the same theater where Robeson appeared in *Show Boat* at night. Their recital consisted of twenty spirituals. "Brown worked incessantly to build up their programmes," wrote their British friend Marie Seton, a journalist. "He searched for music which was within the range of Robeson's voice, or could be moved down to suit his pitch."

Brown was five years older than Robeson and was dedicated to music. Gentle and patient, he was "extremely sensitive to the least variation in Robeson's voice, or his slightest change in mood," recalled Seton. For years before meeting Robeson, Brown had been arranging transcriptions of many little-known and unrecorded spirituals into a traditional folk style.

Robeson discussed the source of the spirituals in an interview with the *Jewish Tribune* after giving a benefit concert for a Jewish organization. "Their text is largely based on the Old Testament," he said. "The Bible was the only form of literature the captive negroes could get at, even those who could read. It was natural for their quick imaginations to find a pathetic similarity between their condition and that of the enslaved Hebrews. . . . They felt that their freedom also would depend on some miracle happening."

But not all the songs in their program were spirituals. A great number were secular and sprang from black people's experiences. Robeson said, "One of the grandest of these is 'Water-Boy,' a song of the negro chain-gangs." When he sang it in his deepest voice, he wanted to make people "know the strong, gallant convict of the chain-gang, make them feel his thirst, understand his naive boasting about his strength."

> *Water boy, where are you hiding?*
> *If you don't come, I'm gonna tell your mammy*
>
> *There ain't no hammer that's on this mountain*
> *That rings like mine, boy, that rings like mine*
> *Done bust this rock, boy, from here to Macon*
> *All the way to the jail, boy, yes, back to the jail*

"Paul took the audience and put it in his pocket with the first song, and kept it there," wrote Essie. People wept as he sang "Water Boy" and "Deep River." Robeson was crying too.

After the first concert on July 3, 1928, the critic from the *Daily Express* said the audience "sat there in a trance of noiseless ecstasy as he

[Robeson] touched our heart-strings with his marvelous voice. . . . We became like little children as we surrendered to his magical genius."

People enjoyed the humor of "Scandalize My Name," and the brisk tempo of "Ezekiel Saw the Wheel," with Brown harmonizing in his tenor baritone voice.

Ezekiel saw the wheel
Yes Lord
Way up in the middle of the air
Ezekiel saw the wheel
Way in the middle of the air
The little wheel runs by faith
And the big wheel runs by the Grace of God

Ezekiel was a biblical prophet who had a vision of God's chariot. Like Ezekiel, Robeson had a vision. He wanted to reach a wider audience outside of America and touch them with the songs of his people. The *Daily Express* critic described Robeson's face "alight and aflame with seership," as he sang. "We saw the rapt mysticism gathering in intensity."

At the end of the program, the audience begged Robeson to sing "Ol' Man River" for an encore. He refused, explaining that since it was part of the show performed at that very theater, he was not allowed to sing it. Finally, though, he gave in, and it became his signature song.

Over the new few weeks, Robeson and Brown recorded a number of the spirituals. With their earnings, the Robesons were able to pay off some of their debts. "It looks as tho at last we are at the end of a long journey," Essie wrote to Van Vechten. "Paul is so happy he grins and jugs."

But after performing in *Show Boat* for nearly a year, and singing "Ol' Man River" night after night, Robeson said he was "bored to death with it." When the show closed in March, he eagerly left for a European concert tour with Brown and Essie.

Robeson wondered if cultured audiences accustomed to classical music by Beethoven and Mozart would like a program of spirituals. One critic suggested that the program of spirituals and work songs was monotonous and that it drew crowds simply because of Robeson's personality. Robeson soon realized that he would need to vary their repertoire and started studying German and French to sing songs from these countries in their native languages.

Their first stop was Vienna, followed by Prague and Budapest. Every concert was sold out. In Budapest, reporters commented on Robeson's "fantastic religiousness." Robeson saw the similarity between Gypsy and Hungarian folk songs and Negro spirituals. "Slav peasant music has a great deal in common with ours," he said, because of suffering "under an alien yoke." A Polish musician pointed out that melodies of Central Africa had influenced European music, and the discovery excited Robeson. With his keen mind, he compared the patterns of folk music in different nationalities.

In the fall of 1929, he and Brown left England for a tour in the United States, starting in New York. The country was suffering from the Great Depression. The stock market on Wall Street had crashed, businesses were failing, and millions were out of work. On November 5, Robeson and Brown gave the first of two concerts at Carnegie Hall. Despite the hard times, advance ticket sales made the concerts a box-office success. The tour wound up at Rutgers, Robeson's alma mater, where fifteen hundred people turned out, "the largest crowd they had ever had at a concert." When the program ended, the audience gave "a college yell and cheer for 'Robey.'"

Robeson's son, Paul Jr., later commented that his father was barely conscious of the "cataclysmic events" of the Depression at that moment. "He lived a pampered, aristocratic life," wrote Paul Jr. Yet, back in London, in the winter of 1930, Robeson was on his way to a gala event when he bumped into a group of unemployed Welsh miners carrying signs and singing. The miners had walked all the way from South Wales

Crowds gather anxiously outside the New York Stock Exchange following the crash of 1929.

to petition the government for help. The Welsh were known worldwide for their exceptional male choirs, and these men were singing and heading for downtown. Robeson immediately joined them. At a large office building, he stood on the steps and sang "Ol' Man River," ballads, and spirituals to lift their spirits. Not only did he pay for their ride home on a freight train, but he also sent them food and clothing, and contributed proceeds from a concert to the Welsh Miners' Relief Fund.

As Robeson scored triumphs with a widening circle of admirers, he retained a sense of awe at his good luck. He briefly kept a diary and jotted down his thoughts. "I don't know what it is . . . that all my life has caused me to succeed whenever I appeared before the public far beyond what my experience, training or knowledge deserved. . . . I shall probably never know my guardian angel." Though he rarely attended church services, or cared about formal religion, he believed that great artists are inspired by God and hold the power to create beauty. Robeson realized that he possessed "some of this power."

"So God watches over me and guides me," he wrote. "He's with me but lets me fight my own battles and hopes I'll win."

chapter 12

one that loved not wisely

—William Shakespeare, *Othello*

Before leaving for the concert tour in America in 1929, Robeson began studying the part of Othello. The Moor of Venice, as Shakespeare described him, referred to a dark-skinned person, perhaps an African or an Arab. Robeson believed that Shakespeare meant the Moor to be "Negro," and had always felt that someday he would act in the play.

Othello is a general in the Venetian Army, secretly married to Desdemona, daughter of a white Venetian senator. When her father finds out, he is enraged. Othello's ensign, Iago, angry because Othello passed over him for a promotion, seeks revenge. He convinces Othello that Desdemona has betrayed him by taking another lover, and Othello kills Desdemona. Moments before she dies, Othello realizes he's been duped. Authorities arrive to arrest him and he says,

> When you shall these unlucky deeds relate,
> Speak of me as I am. . . .
> Of one that lov'd not wisely but too well.

Faced with the shame of having murdered his innocent wife, Othello kills himself.

Robeson said, "I feel the play is so modern, for the problem is the problem of my own people. It is a tragedy of racial conflict, a tragedy of honor rather than of jealousy." White actors usually portrayed the

Robeson in the London production of *Othello*, with Peggy Ashcroft, 1930

character by darkening their skin with makeup. But Robeson said, "When a negro does any good work as an actor every one begins to talk of Othello. Of course, I think about Othello, but as a sort of culmination." "I think I'll wait till I've had more experience in the theatre," he told Essie.

One night, he asked her, "Do you really think I could play Othello now, if I worked at it?"

103

"I know you can, silly," she replied.

"All right," he said, "I'll do it." So he signed a contract to star in a London production scheduled for spring 1930.

He would be the first black actor to star in *Othello* since Ira Aldridge who had performed the role in Europe a century earlier. Aldridge, an African American from New York, had emigrated to England to study acting and further his career.

"Here is a part that has dignity for a Negro actor," Robeson said later in a film interview. "Often we don't get those opportunities. My people will be very proud."

To prepare for *Othello*, Robeson read all of Shakespeare's plays. He listened to recordings and studied pronunciation. "I had to work on that very hard," he said. In a text printed in Old English, Robeson discovered that many words were spelled differently in Shakespeare's time. "Chance," for example, was written as "chaunce," and "demand" as "demaunde," and had to be pronounced properly.

Robeson thought about the character of Othello in a racial context. "The fact that he's from Africa is very clear to me," he said. "Shakespeare posed this problem of a Black man in a white society." As Robeson told his friend Marie Seton, he imagined Othello "moving like a panther." Robeson went to the London Zoo and watched the panthers for hours, so he could imitate their movements. As an athlete, Robeson had command over his muscular body, and understood how to use it to express emotion.

The producer cast himself as Iago, Othello's devious friend, and chose his wife Nellie to be the director. Neither had any experience mounting a Shakespearean play. When rehearsals began in London in April 1930, Robeson knew they were in trouble. Nellie sat in the first row of the dress circle yelling commands through a megaphone.

Essie attended every rehearsal and wrote in her diary, "Nellie doesn't know what it is all about. Talks of . . . the 'flow' and 'austere beauty,' a lot of parlor junk, which means nothing. . . . She can't even get actors from one side of the stage to the other. Poor Paul is lost." All the cast members suffered under Nellie's incompetent direction. The actors tried to solve the problem by secretly rehearsing at each other's houses in the evenings.

One time, Robeson asked Nellie a question and she shouted through the megaphone, "Mr. Robeson, there are other people on the stage besides yourself!" Robeson's costar, Peggy Ashcroft, who played the part of Othello's wife Desdemona, was horrified by Nellie's rudeness. Ashcroft was just twenty-two and was thrilled to be performing with Robeson, age thirty-two. "For us young people in England at the time [Robeson] was a great figure, and we all had his records," she recalled. During rehearsals, Ashcroft became romantically involved with Robeson. "How could one not fall in love in such a situation with such a man?" she said. The drama itself made their affair "inevitable."

On May 30, 1930, the play opened at the Savoy Theatre. Robeson was "wild with nerves," wrote Essie. Her own hair "went gray in a patch" as she watched the final days of rehearsal. Nellie placed the actors far back from the audience where they couldn't be heard. For the climactic final scene, which takes place in Othello and Desdemona's bedchamber, Nellie put the bed in a dark corner of the stage, so the emotional impact was lost. She allowed the set designer to create a huge four-poster, which made such a racket when it was hoisted into position behind the curtain that the actors told the stagehands not to move the bed until they had finished their lines.

To make matters worse, Nellie insisted that Robeson wear an Elizabethan costume of tights and doublets in Act 1 instead of a Moor's robes. The costume was true to the time when Shakespeare had written the play, but it wasn't right for the tragedy. On opening night, Robeson was stiff and subdued. He said he "started off with my performance pitched a bit higher than I wanted it to be." Yet, by the final scene when he killed Desdemona and then stabbed himself, he moved the audience with his passion.

The "frenzy of applause subsided" only after twenty curtain calls. "Robeson! Robeson! Speech! Speech!" shouted the audience. He stepped forward and said, "I took the part of Othello with much fear. Now I am so happy."

Reviews for Robeson ranged from raves to lukewarm praise. Some critics hailed him as "magnificent" and "remarkable." Others described his performance as "disappointing." Many agreed that he had played the role as a "thoughtful, kindly man, civilised and cultured," rather than as a "great soldier." Ashcroft received "glowing notices." But critics slammed the producer and director for their appalling production. "They caught the hell they so well deserved," noted Essie. After the stinging reviews, the producer who had played the part of Iago "fled like a frightened rabbit" and turned his part over to his understudy.

Robeson focused on improving his performance. "He has been working steadily at his part," wrote Essie, "and some changes have been made in his costumes, so that he is 100 percent better." Nevertheless, the show did not attract a wide audience and closed six weeks after opening. For the next few months, the company toured outlying cities.

Robeson understood the criticisms about his acting technique. Yet he told a reporter that taking the role had liberated him. "*Othello* has taken away from me all kinds of fears, all sense of limitation, and all racial prejudice," he said. "*Othello* has opened to me new and wider fields; in a word, *Othello* has made me free." Thirteen years later, he performed *Othello* on Broadway in New York with a deeper understanding of his character. The final monologue was added to his concert program of spirituals.

When reporters asked Ashcroft how she felt about being kissed "by a coloured man" in some scenes, she replied, "Of course I do not mind! I see no difference in being kissed by Paul Robeson and being kissed by any other man. It is just necessary to the play. For myself I look on it as a privilege to act with a great artist like Paul Robeson." There was a difference, though, because of their feelings for one another.

When Essie discovered a love letter from Ashcroft to Robeson, she was furious. Humiliated. She stormed off to Territet, Switzerland, to join her mother and son. Essie had sent them there for the baby's health. Paul Jr., at age two and a half, had become terribly sick with tonsillitis and stomach cramps during the run of *Othello*, and Essie had thought the Swiss mountain air would be good for him.

Now she wrote angry, bitter letters to Robeson. He was touring the English provinces with Brown in a new kind of concert program. One half consisted of scenes from *The Emperor Jones*, and the second part was devoted to spirituals and a song by Beethoven. He wanted freedom as an artist and in his personal life. Essie accused him of being a cheating husband, "a rotten parent," and "a dishonest artist."

"He must have been lying to me for five years," she wrote. "I am surely a jackass if ever there was one."

Although the future seemed uncertain, Essie developed into a glamorous independent woman in the early 1930s. She won praise for her acting with Robeson in a silent movie — *Borderline* — filmed before he performed in *Othello*.

Robeson responded calmly. He wrote that he was sorry she had read the letter. "I must have a certain amount of privacy in my life," he explained. He suggested that he and Essie remain apart for a while. She could stay in Switzerland and he might come to visit her and Paul Jr. before leaving on a scheduled concert tour. "Love to the boy," he added. "Do tell me about him and how he's going along. Of course I'm interested."

Robeson was primarily concerned with his career and their financial situation. "We'll need every penny, and I'll be so busy with my work, I'll not be able to see much of you," he wrote. "I am in a period of transition. . . . I would like to get on with my work. . . . Let's hope all will come out right."

Robeson's letter made Essie livid. She wrote that he was "secret, mean, low." Would she end their marriage? After years of loving him, taking care of him, supporting him in every way to develop his potential and further his career, Essie faced a crisis.

sometimes i'm up, sometimes i'm down

— "Nobody Knows the Trouble I've Seen"

By December 1930, Robeson temporarily joined Essie, Paul Jr., and Grandma Goode in Switzerland to celebrate Christmas. Essie was willing to see him. Though still angry, she had not closed the door on the possibility of them getting together again. Yet their values clashed. She was materialistic. He was an artist, a free spirit, and did not want to be controlled. Money and possessions didn't matter to him. Independent and strong, Essie had been working on her own projects, including a biography about her husband titled *Paul Robeson, Negro*. They never discussed it and she didn't show him the manuscript. When Robeson read the book, he was furious because she had made up so many stories and mischaracterized him as lazy, helpless, and dependent on her. The book even commented on his flaws as a father, quoting Grandma Goode as saying, "Paul saw far too little of his baby."

The book was published the day after the opening of *Othello*, before Essie had found out about her husband's romance with Ashcroft. That affair had ended, but now he was crazy about another woman, Yolande Jackson, an Englishwoman from a wealthy family. Their romance had deepened into love, and he planned to marry her. Yolande, an aspiring actress, was warm and playful, with a great sense of humor. Her personality enchanted Robeson.

Essie said, "At first, naturally, I was very upset about it all." Then she said, "I certainly hope he gets what he wants." Essie agreed to give

109

him a divorce, but then changed her mind. She wanted to stay Mrs. Paul Robeson. From time to time, they saw each other, and they kept in touch through letters. Friends warned him that if he left Essie and married Yolande, a white woman, it would offend people of both races and hurt his career.

With Robeson no longer around, Essie formed new friendships and pursued her interest in writing. She traveled to South Carolina to research a novel based on the lives of her mother and grandmother. And she planned to visit Africa. Essie began to see this period of separation as an opportunity for growth.

Robeson returned to America in January 1931 for a coast-to-coast concert tour with Brown. Even when they weren't living together, Essie cared about him: "I do so hope he had another great success," she wrote to the Van Vechtens. To vary his program, Robeson had added German lieder (poems set to music). As a linguist, he had been enthusiastic about studying German to understand the poems.

Critics complained about the "art songs." They misunderstood Robeson's intentions and said that he was presenting the lieder to please "more intelligent" young black people who dismissed spirituals as "something beneath their new pride in their race." Robeson said that black artists "ought to do as many things as they can do well." Brown wrote to Essie that "nothing was going according to plan."

"Is he fed up," she asked Brown, "is he bored, is he angry? Has he lost interest in his work?" Robeson wrote to Essie, "What I really need is about 3 months out to do nothing but learn new songs."

In the spring, he sailed to London to begin rehearsing a Eugene O'Neill play, *The Hairy Ape*. The story told of a stoker, Yank Smith, who shovels coal on a transatlantic liner under brutal conditions. When a wealthy passenger sees him in the stokehold and looks at him in horror, she faints. The part was usually performed by a white actor, but Robeson thought the play had possibilities for him. However, he later said, "The rehearsals nearly killed me. I am supposed to be a strong man. Yet I couldn't stand up to the strain on my physical strength." The first act required Robeson to feed the furnace while shouting and snarling in fury.

Essie attended the dress rehearsal and worried. "He is using much too much voice," she said, "and if he keeps on like this, he will strain it." Nonetheless, Robeson was "magnificent" on opening night. He performed the role stripped to the waist, and his muscular body caused a sensation.

Five days later, the play suddenly closed. As Essie had predicted, Robeson had laryngitis and "no voice at all." Suffering from exhaustion and strained nerves, he spent a week in a nursing home. When reporters asked him about his future plans, he said he would not act for a few years.

Upon recovering, Robeson devoted himself to learning Russian so that he could sing songs in that language. Studying with a Russian composer, Robeson said that the music suited his voice. "There is a kinship between the Russians and the Negroes," he told the press. "They were both serfs," enslaved laborers, and the music expressed their sadness. Robeson planned to introduce two Russian songs into his program. The composer of one of these, "The Captive," dedicated the piece to Robeson.

Without Essie looking after him, Robeson's health deteriorated. In November 1931, he came down with influenza, and at the last minute, he cancelled a sold-out concert at Royal Albert Hall. The huge concert hall in London was a world-famous venue for musical performances, like Carnegie Hall in New York. Thousands of angry ticket holders refused to go home, expecting Robeson to act like a professional and carry on despite having the flu. Even Brown was annoyed with his behavior.

Essie sympathized. "Paul is behaving very, very strangely," she wrote. "Poor fellow, I'm sorry for him." He couldn't make up his mind about his work or his private life. Although Robeson wanted to be free, he was tired and unhappy and missed Essie, as he told her in his letters. "He wanted to share his intellectual and artistic life with her,"

Robeson signs his autograph for an admiring fan after a concert in 1930.

Desperate men, out of work or too poor to pay their bills, line up to receive free bread at the
McCauley Water Street Mission under the Brooklyn Bridge in New York, in the 1930s.

—something he couldn't do with Yolande. Essie worried that he would lose his place as an international star by publicly flaunting his love affair. In December, Robeson spent Christmas in London with Essie, Paul Jr., and Grandma Goode. Paul Jr. later wrote that he and his father "played together happily" all day before Robeson sailed to New York for another concert tour.

At Town Hall in New York, the audience enthusiastically applauded Robeson's performance of the Russian songs. A dash of humor was added to the program by Brown's new arrangement of "There's No Hidin' Place Down There." The song about a "sinner man" who can't go to heaven because of his misdeeds struck close to home, given his situation with Essie. Reporters hounded him with questions about their separation—were they going to get a divorce? Essie kept changing her mind; Paul was also unsure.

> There's no hidin' place down there
> There's no hidin' place down there
> Oh, I went to the rock to hide my face
> The rock cried out "No hidin' place"
> There's no hidin' place down there.

In May 1932, Robeson starred in a revival of *Show Boat* in New York. By now, the Great Depression had worsened. Breadlines and soup kitchens sprang up in cities and towns throughout the country and served free meals to hungry men, women, and children. Most people couldn't afford food, much less theater tickets. Still, everyone craved entertainment to help them forget their troubles for a little while.

Edna Ferber, the author of *Show Boat*, predicted that "no one would come to see it" so soon after the original Broadway production in 1927. At first, she announced that she would not attend the opening on May 19 at the Casino Theater, but at the last minute changed her mind. When she arrived, a riot seemed to be going on. Ferber said, "I immediately decided that infuriated ticket purchasers were already demanding their money back." Although the performance had already started, a line had formed at the box office, and the man working there was saying, "NOMORESEATSNOMORESEATSNOMORESEATSNOMORE-SEATS."

Ferber stepped inside and stood at the back of the theater, just as Robeson made his entrance. "In all my years of going to the theatre," she wrote, "I never have seen an ovation like that given any figure of the stage, the concert hall, or the opera." When he sang "Ol' Man River," he stopped the show, and "they called him back again and again." The *New York Herald Tribune* described Robeson's voice as "celestial." The *New York Times* wrote, "Mr. Robeson has a touch of genius. It is not merely his voice . . . It is his understanding that gives 'Ol' Man River' an epic lift."

Robeson's success led to guest appearances on radio programs. He tried to offer his audiences "not only an artistic gift but a spiritual one as well." Robeson said, "When singing for the Radio, I . . . go close [to the microphone] and sing quite softly to it, as if I were alone with a friend."

In a letter to Essie telling her about his successful concerts, he wrote, "This country is *really* mine. And strange, I like it again and deeply. After all—this audience understands the Negro in a way impossible for Europeans."

Robeson, at the peak of his success, was in a position to help others. He gave a midnight benefit performance of *Show Boat* for the Harlem Children's Aid Society, and a concert at an outdoor stadium for a crowd of 9,000. One of his most gratifying moments came when Rutgers awarded him an honorary Master of Arts degree at its June commencement. Robeson, who was thirty-four, called the event "the greatest hour of my short life." Rutgers President Robert Clothier praised Robeson for excelling at the college "despite cruel race prejudice." Robeson believed that this recognition would help to give his people "confidence and self-respect."

In September, Robeson left *Show Boat* to return to London and marry

Yolande. He had made up his mind, and Essie accepted his decision. She wrote, "Paul and I are great friends, and I think we like each other much better now than we ever did." But later that month, Yolande broke off the relationship because of pressure from her conservative, upper-class family. They disapproved of her marrying a black man, even a celebrity like Robeson who was greatly respected and admired in England. Their reaction made her aware of the difficulties that might lie ahead.

Yolande's rejection devastated Robeson. For weeks, he refused to see anyone. But he had also come to the conclusion that marrying her would be a mistake. Her superior, snobbish attitude toward her chauffeur and Indian servants had always bothered him. He came from a working-class family and community and identified with them.

By the end of October, he invited Essie to his hotel for tea and told her to stop divorce proceedings. They had a long talk and decided to work things out. He moved into the "flat" (apartment) on fashionable Buckingham Street with Essie, Paul Jr., and Grandma Goode, and Essie started to plan "the beginning of a new life together."

Paul Jr. remembered spending his fifth birthday with his parents. "I enjoyed long talks with my father," he recalled. "One of my first and best memories of him comes from this week, when he took me to see *Peter Pan* . . . and softly talked me through the scary parts, holding my hand and helping me deal with my fear of Captain Hook and the crocodile."

Newspaper photographers snapped a picture of Robeson and eight-year-old Paul in England in 1936. At that time, Robeson began calling his son "Chappie."

115

feel the spirit

—"Every Time I Feel the Spirit"

Paul Jr. wrote that his parents worked together again "as a professional team," discussing Robeson's career options and programs. However, Robeson's lawyer Bob Rockmore was now his manager and controlled the finances and contracts. The new arrangement gave Robeson the freedom he needed.

On December 5, 1932, he jotted a note to himself: "Am terribly happy at No. 19 [Buckingham Street—their flat] . . . *I feel so ambitious. Want to work all day* at something." He was adding songs in Russian, German, French, Dutch, Hungarian, Turkish, and Hebrew to his repertoire. At home, he listened to records. "Unquestionably Russian songs are right—most right for me," he said, because he felt an emotional connection to them.

Bursting with new ideas, he was also eager to learn African languages. In January 1933, he and Essie enrolled at the University of London. He did comparative work in African linguistics, while she took courses in anthropology with a focus on African cultures. Robeson talked of visiting Africa. "I am proud of my African descent," he told an interviewer.

"I am learning Swahili, Tivi, and other African dialects—which come easily to me *because their rhythm is the same as that employed by the American Negro in speaking English.*" When he started studying West Coast dialects, such as Ewe, Efik, and Hausa, he heard sounds he recalled from childhood. The pitch and pattern of tones reminded him of the "Negro

English" dialect that was spoken when he was a boy. It was "like a home-coming," he said. Robeson was excited about discovering his heritage and wanted to inspire black people to feel the same pride. Culture, he believed, would express black values and bring about change.

He agreed to do a revival of O'Neill's play *All God's Chillun Got Wings*. It came about when actress Flora Robson moved into a flat across the hall from the Robesons and they all became good friends. Robeson recreated his role as the black law student in this London production. Flora Robson took the part of his racist white wife. Robson had trained at the Royal Academy of Dramatic Art in London, and in 1931 she joined the prestigious Old Vic Theatre Company. The Old Vic was a not-for-profit theater that put on Shakespearean plays as well as operas, ballets, and artistic experiments. Robeson thought that working with such an accomplished actress would be a learning experience for him—and it was.

Robeson and Flora Robson in a scene from the 1933 London production of *All God's Chillun Got Wings*

He was so dedicated to the project that he agreed to take a lower salary than usual of only ten pounds (fifty dollars) for the entire run of the show. *Chillun* opened at the Embassy Theatre on March 12, 1933. "People almost fought to get seats," recalled his friend, Marie Seton. The run was extended, and every performance was sold out, even the standing room area. The director marveled at the way the two stars connected onstage. "A perfect dramatic partnership," wrote the *Observer*. A reviewer for the *News-Chronicle* said, "Flora Robson . . . makes you forget she is acting. Of Paul Robeson, I am never sure if he is acting, but is just himself." Robeson took criticism seriously. Despite any praise he received, he realized that he had "a long way to go on the painful journey from performing actor to theatrical artist."

Social problems also concerned Robeson. The Great Depression had spread to the United Kingdom, where it was known as the Great Slump. More than three million people lost their jobs and depended on doles, payments they received from local governments. Industrial areas were especially hard hit. Robeson had performed *Othello* in these towns and knew the people. As a younger actor touring with Mrs. Campbell's repertory company, he had stayed in workers' homes. In Manchester, a textile center, he spoke with a worker whose father and grandfather had woven cotton picked by enslaved people in America. The workers had supported abolishing slavery during the Civil War. Robeson thought about these ties with British laborers. He had sung with unemployed Welsh miners and connected with them. "My whole social and political development was in England," he said years later.

In London, he had met outspoken socialists, such as H. G. Wells. Listening to Wells in 1933, Robeson heard new ideas about a society that would abolish class distinctions, and an economic system in which workers would share profits cooperatively. he said he had "never really thought about Socialism," said Robeson. The theories appealed to him.

While *Chillun* ran at the Piccadilly (where it transferred from the Embassy Theater), several thousand Jews landed in London as refugees

At an exhibition of twentieth-century German art in London, Paul Robeson and Larry Brown perform in aid of German artists banned by Hitler. A triptych, *Reflecting Darkness* by Max Beckmann, hangs on the wall behind the piano.

from Nazi Germany. Adolph Hitler had become Chancellor of Germany and had started attacks on Jews, communists, homosexuals, Jehovah's Witnesses, and the Roma people (often called Gypsies), labeling them enemies of the state. On April 1, 1933, he passed laws banning Jews from businesses, professions, the arts, and schools. German Jews fled in fear of being beaten to death or imprisoned.

Marie Seton asked Robeson to help the refugees by giving a benefit performance of *Chillun*. At first, he refused, saying "I'm an artist. . . . I don't understand politics. I've avoided controversies." But then he mulled it over and thought about how the plight of Jews in Germany was like that of African Americans, as captured in "Go Down, Moses"—Let *my people* go. He had always understood the meaning of those words.

119

Robeson agreed to perform a special matinee of *Chillun*, with which the actors raised two thousand pounds (about ten thousand dollars) for the refugees. Later, Robeson said that this was his first political act as an artist.

Chillun closed because Robeson had committed to shoot a film version of O'Neill's play *The Emperor Jones*. In May 1933, he and Essie traveled to New York for the production. "Talkies" (movies with sound) were new, and for the first time, his voice would be heard in a movie.

Robeson, playing Brutus Jones, a chain gang prisoner, tries to escape in the movie version of *The Emperor Jones*.

Although part of *Jones* was set in Georgia, Robeson insisted that he would not film in the segregated South. Spoken as well as unspoken Jim Crow laws prevailed in the southern states. Black people could not occupy the same sidewalk as white people, and they had to step off the curb when they passed a white person. Racial violence had increased during the Great Depression. White people competed for jobs usually held by minorities and in some cases murdered black workers in order to take their places. In 1933, the number of lynchings surged from eight to twenty-eight in a total of eleven states, including California, Maryland, and Missouri. Most lynchings were prompted by accusations that black men had insulted white men, or tried to register to vote, or simply looked at or spoke to a white woman. An alleged crime was enough to drive a mob to a public act of racial terrorism. Women were lynched too, such as the Alabama schoolteacher who scolded white children when they threw rocks at her.

Given these circumstances, Robeson held firm and refused to film the movie in the South. The producer begged him to reconsider, asking Robeson to at least shoot the jungle scenes in Charleston, South Carolina. At first, Robeson agreed to do it if he could stay in the best hotel in Charleston. But the manager said, "If I allow a Negro in this hotel, I might as well burn it down." So Robeson filmed *Jones* at New York's old Paramount Studio Complex in Astoria, Queens. The producers built an artificial jungle and swamp and heated the water so that Robeson wouldn't catch one of his frequent colds. For the scene depicting Jones in a prison chain gang, Robeson, bare-chested and shackled, "busts" rocks as he sings "Water Boy," a plaintive song he performed in concerts.

Photographer Edward Steichen took twenty-six pictures of Robeson in his Emperor Jones costume, a military jacket with epaulettes, braid, and shiny brass buttons. In one of the images, Steichen captured a brooding, dark look on Robeson's face—"defiance mixed with fear." The iconic picture appeared in the August 1933 issue of *Vanity Fair* and led to movie offers from several Hollywood studios. Robeson turned them down. He felt that Hollywood wanted to portray only the "plantation

In his role as the Emperor Jones, Robeson glowers menacingly. This photo by Edward Steichen became an iconic image, exhibited in museums throughout the country.

122

type of Negro." Robeson intended to do "human stories," if only he could find one, but good roles for a black actor were difficult to find.

The *Emperor Jones* movie was released in September at two New York theaters, the Rivoli, for white people, and the Roosevelt in Harlem for black audiences. It was a breakthrough. For the first time, a black actor played the lead in a full-length, mainstream "talking" picture. Critics applauded performances by Robeson and the cast, but members of the black community attacked the film for using the 'n-word'. The *Amsterdam News* condemned Robeson for agreeing to perform in the movie. "O'Neill does not know Negroes," stated the critic. *"The Emperor Jones* struck me . . . as being written for morons." Robeson defended O'Neill's script: "Coming from the pen of a white man it's an almost incredible achievement, without a false note in the characterization."

In January 1934, Robeson returned to concertizing, and he and Brown began a long tour through England. Aside from spirituals, Robeson sang Russian, Hebrew, Mexican, English, and Scottish folk songs. For him, the songs of these different lands shared a "common humanity," in expressing the universal human emotions of delight, tenderness, protest, and the pain of suffering and loss.

When he returned home in April, Essie read a letter she had received from composer George Gershwin, who had written hit Broadway musicals as well as classical compositions. He had heard Robeson sing at parties. Gershwin was working on a folk opera, *Porgy and Bess*. "I have had Paul in mind for the part of Porgy," he wrote, "which I think suits him admirably. I am bearing in mind Paul's voice in writing it, and if there are some things which are out of his range, I am sure I can fix it up." If Robeson had accepted the role, he would have broken the color barrier by being been the first black opera singer in America. But he declined Gershwin's offer. He knew his voice wasn't suited to operatic music, and he was determined to reach a broad popular audience, not just opera lovers.

Robeson kept looking for a movie project that would convey a true picture of African culture. That summer, director Zoltan Korda asked him to play an African chief, Bosambo, in an adventure movie, *Sanders of the River*. Korda had spent four months in Central Africa filming dances and rituals, and Robeson thought the footage was "magnificent." Korda planned to use the footage throughout the movie. Robeson was especially excited about Korda's recordings of African music. The music revealed "much more melody than I've ever heard come out of Africa," said Robeson. "And I think the Americans will be amazed to find how many of their modern dance steps are relics of an African heritage."

A still from the movie *Sanders of the River,* with Robeson in the starring role of Bosambo

Robeson took the part. But when he read the script, he realized that it presented a favorable view of British colonialism. In 1934, the United Kingdom still ruled many colonies throughout the world: India, Hong

Kong, West Africa, South Africa, Jamaica, and the Bahamas. Although Robeson condemned the practice of European whites ruling people of color, he chose to do the film because it allowed him to portray an African character with a real African background.

The story takes place in British Nigeria, and centers on Bosambo, an educated tribal chief. Bosambo works with Sanders, a British river officer, to calm rebellious natives. But native warriors turn on Bosambo. Sanders rescues him and appoints him as the new king of the tribes. At the end, Bosambo, clad only in a leopard-skin loincloth and an ivory-tusk necklace, sings the "Canoe Song" as Sanders sails away. Robeson recorded the number, which became a popular hit.

Production began in the summer of 1934 at the Shepperton Studios, just outside London. Korda hired 400 black people, mostly Africans, as extras. Robeson enjoyed working with them and hearing their different languages. One day, he overheard a man speaking in his native language, and to his amazement, he understood what the man was saying. "I spoke to him at once," recalled Robeson, "he was from the Ibo tribe in Nigeria—the very tribe and country from which my own father's family came. Surely I must have heard a word or two of this language that had crept into my father's speech and that he himself had inherited." Robeson was thrilled. He told a reporter, "For the first time since I began acting, I feel that I've found my place in the world, that there's something out of my own culture which I can express and perhaps help to preserve."

During the weeks of filming, Robeson often took Paul Jr., age seven, to the set. "He taught me games of all kinds, told me stories, and stimulated my intellectual curiosity," recalled Paul Jr. "I remember him as surprisingly playful for one who appeared on the surface to be so serious." When they arrived at the studio, Paul Jr. observed his father's "natural ease, making himself accessible to everyone. He was a popular superstar who belonged to the outside world, yet behaved like a regular person."

But the final version of the film bitterly disappointed Robeson because it glorified British colonialism more than it had in the original script. During the last five days of shooting, an imperialist angle had been added without his knowledge or permission. He had expected to star in a serious film that presented the dignity of African culture. Instead, the movie was trite and corny.

At the premiere of the film at the Leicester Square Theatre, he was so angry he slipped out. According to one account, Essie went after him and persuaded him to return. When the screening ended, a piano was pushed onto the stage and he was asked to sing. Robeson refused in protest and later said, "I personally am sorry about doing *Sanders*," and "I hate the picture."

The reviews made him angrier. The London *Sunday Times* noted that *Sanders* provided "a grand insight into our special English difficulties in the governing of savage races." Black people were portrayed as "childlike and superstitious." When the black press criticized him for lending his name and prestige to a movie that patronized Africans, Essie defended him and said, "Look, we have to make money."

However, Robeson took full responsibility for having made a mistake in trusting Korda and vowed never to work with him again. Robeson tried but failed to buy the rights to the movie and all the prints, to prevent distribution. The movie turned out to be a success at the box office, but Robeson donated his earnings: "All money earned from *Sanders* went to help Africa."

Slowly, Robeson was becoming aware of the world around him and his ability to make changes. "It is not as imitation Europeans, but as Africans, that we have a value," he wrote. "To remind the world that a Negro has something to offer, Paul Robeson will act and sing."

no second class aboard this train

chapter 15

— "Get on Board, Little Children"

While Robeson was filming *Sanders of the River*, Russian filmmaker Sergei Eisenstein invited him to come to the Soviet Union. By now, 1934, Robeson was an international celebrity. Eisenstein wanted to discuss the possibility of making a film with Robeson about Toussaint L'Ouverture, an enslaved black man who led a revolt in the late eighteenth century that defeated Napoleon's troops and liberated the French colony of Haiti. Toussaint's father had been an African prince captured by slavers. The fact that an enslaved black man could achieve this military victory "was proof of African genius," said Eisenstein.

Although he thought Robeson would be perfect for the film, official approval had not yet been given by the head of the Soviet film industry. Eisenstein had fallen out of favor with Josef Stalin, the leader of the communist government. In the early 1930s, Eisenstein had stayed away from the Soviet Union, filming in Hollywood and Mexico, and Stalin accused him of plotting to defect. But Eisenstein had high hopes and contacted Robeson through their mutual friend, Marie Seton, who helped arrange a trip to Moscow. Since it was their first visit, the Robesons asked Seton to go with them because she had been there before.

On December 20, 1934, Robeson, Essie, and Seton left London for Moscow, stopping in Berlin for a one-day layover. They found the city to be very different than in 1930 when he was performing in *The Emperor Jones*. They had enjoyed the city then. In spite of Nazi rallies, Robeson

At Waterloo Station in London, Robeson and Essie are about to board a train.

Nazi storm troopers march through Berlin as civilians salute
from their windows and wave German flags.

seemed unaware of the impending menace, probably because Nazis were a minority, and Adolph Hitler was regarded as a political fanatic not to be taken seriously.

But in 1933, Hitler and the Nazis had taken complete control of Germany and changed many laws. They suspended civil rights, such as freedom of speech, and began an anti-Semitic campaign as well as attacks on progressive people such as communists and labor union members. Hitler's mission was to systematically eliminate Jews by sending them to concentration camps to be killed. He also despised people of color and regarded them as racially inferior, a threat to the purity of the Germanic race. Hitler charged that Jews had brought black people into Germany through their involvement with jazz and swing music.

Now, wrote Essie, their one day in Berlin was a "nightmare." Nazi storm troopers (Hitler's private army) glared menacingly at Robeson and muttered racial slurs as he, Essie, and Seton walked from the railroad station to the hotel. Robeson knew German and understood the words. "It was like seeing the Ku Klux Klan in power," said Robeson. "Brown shirts instead of white sheets, but the same idea."

A musician that the Robesons met on their earlier trip to Berlin came to the hotel to see them. Nervously, he told them about the persecution of the Jews and communists, and the horrors of the concentration camps. Communists had staged a protest against Hitler's government, and the leaders were imprisoned, shot, and hanged. The visitor said he wanted to walk in the streets while he talked. "Paul said he did not want to go out," recalled Seton, so she and Essie went with the man. When they returned, Robeson was sitting near the window, gazing down into the street. "Even his back had a brooding look," wrote Seton. Finally he said, "I feel I need a bath!"

"He strode across the room, his movements like a lion seeking a means to escape its cage," wrote Seton. "When he came back his anger had turned to deliberation." Robeson remembered that Seton had asked him to do a matinee benefit performance in London for the wretched

German refugees. He said to Seton, "I thought you . . . were exaggerating at the time." But he realized that the musician who had just visited had given an accurate account of conditions in Germany. "You know what this racism means in my case?" said Robeson. "We shouldn't be on the streets more than necessary." He understood clearly the Nazi anti-black policy. That was why he hadn't gone out with their visitor. Essie was light-skinned and could pass as a white woman. They decided to eat at the hotel and wait until it was time to leave that night.

When they arrived at the station to catch their train, Essie went to organize the luggage. Robeson and Seton stood on the platform talking. Storm troopers armed with revolvers surrounded them and stared. Seton was terrified. Robeson told her to stay calm. "This is like Mississippi," he said quietly. "It's how a lynching begins. If either of us moves, or shows fear, they'll go further. We must keep our heads."

Seton recalled that Robeson's expression changed from "fear" to "fury." When Essie joined them, a second line of storm troopers formed behind her. "They think you are both German women," muttered Robeson. A black man couldn't be seen talking to white German women. In the distance, they heard their train coming, but they still didn't have their luggage. As soon as the train pulled in, Robeson ordered, "Get on!" The Nazis didn't stop them as they jumped aboard. A porter rushed down the platform with a trolley and threw their baggage onto the train.

For a long while, Robeson sat in their compartment, looking out the window. After the train finally crossed the border from Germany into Poland, he relaxed. "I never understood what Fascism was before," he said. "I'll fight it wherever I find it from now on." Fascism had begun in Italy with dictator Benito Mussolini. The danger of rule by white supremacists like Mussolini and Hitler, who both believed in a master race, marked a turning point in Robeson's life.

the fare is cheap and all can go

— "Get on Board, Little Children"

On December 23, the Robesons and Seton arrived in Moscow, receiving a warm welcome from Eisenstein and Essie's younger brothers John and Frank. John, who had immigrated to Moscow a year earlier, was an auto mechanic and had a job as a bus driver at the Foreign Workers' Club. Frank, a powerfully built man, had just arrived in the Soviet Union and planned to join the Russian circus as a member of the wrestling team. Essie had stayed in touch with her brothers through letters. John had written that although everyday items such as underwear, typing paper, and brooms were not available, no Jim Crow segregation was present in the Soviet Union. Robeson had heard and read similar reports from American friends who had visited Russia. Black people were treated like honored guests—and he and Essie found it to be true.

Right away, Robeson and Eisenstein chatted in Russian like two old friends. "I find it much easier to speak Russian than any other language," said Robeson. "It seems more expressive of my feelings." That first night after dinner and the theater, Robeson and Eisenstein stayed up late discussing their passion for languages and music. Robeson had brought his gramophone and records of his own spirituals, as well as music from Africa, China, and Thailand. These records were impossible to get in Russia and Robeson wanted to share them. He and Eisenstein played them over and over again, analyzing the rhythms.

Filmmaker Sergei Eisenstein (on the right) greets Robeson at the Belorussky Railway Station in Moscow, December 1934. Actor and director Herbert Marshall (in the middle), who was studying with Eisenstein, joins in the welcome.

During the next two weeks, the Robesons and Seton were wined and dined. Although Robeson did not give any concerts, he sang on many occasions. At a Christmas Eve dinner, everyone feasted on turkey and caviar, and guests danced the tango and the Irish jig. To everyone's amusement, Eisenstein demonstrated dance steps he *thought* he had learned at the Savoy Ballroom in Harlem. After the guests refreshed themselves with Russian tea, Robeson said, "I would like to sing some of my people's Psalms," which included "Go Down, Moses."

Robeson moved the Russians, as he had Americans and Europeans, with the spirituals, which he knew might be considered subversive. He said, "The Russians have experienced many of the same things the American Negroes have experienced." Before Robeson arrived in Russia, the All Soviet Broadcasting Committee had played his recording of "Steal Away," but then apologized to listeners because the communist government had banned religion. The *London Times* reported the incident. The Soviet press characterized Robeson's intentions of singing spirituals as a protest against the treatment of black people in America, a capitalist country.

At a party held at a club for people in the movie industry, Robeson gave a short speech in Russian and sang an aria acapella from the Russian opera *Boris Godunov*. People rushed to embrace him and called him Pavelushka, "dearest, beloved little Paul." He also performed several songs including "Ol' Man River," which the audience lovingly dubbed "Meesseesseeppee."

Robeson also sang spirituals for the workers at a factory in Moscow. He explained that despite the religious language of the spirituals, they were protest songs about a people's struggle for freedom. He observed that the laborers in the factory were men of color who came from outlying regions of the Soviet Union—Chinese, Manchurians, Uzbeks, Mongolians, and Jews—yet accomplished their tasks side by side, as equals.

When a reporter for the *Daily Worker*, a Communist Party newspaper based in New York, asked him if he had noticed a race problem in the Soviet Union, Robeson chuckled, replying, "Only that it seems to work to my advantage!" "I was not prepared for the happiness I see on every face in Moscow. . . . I was not prepared for the endless friendliness, which surrounded me from the moment I crossed the border. . . . This joy and happiness and friendliness . . . is all the more keenly felt by me because of the day I spent in Berlin on the way here, and that was a day of horror —in an atmosphere of hatred, fear and suspicion. . . . This is home to me. I feel more kinship to the Russian people under their new society than I ever felt anywhere else."

Like many idealistic visitors, including black friends from Harlem, Robeson caught the upbeat spirit in Moscow. Foreign visitors were given carefully arranged tours to leave them with a good impression. Robeson was blind to Josef Stalin's crimes and didn't know that his program to industrialize and modernize the Soviet Union had caused raging famine in Ukraine.

In the early 1930s, Josef Stalin, leader of the Soviet Union's communist government, was considered by many to be the head of a society where everyone would be equal. But he was just starting to launch his wave of political purges known as the Great Terror.

Stalin, leader of the communist government, ruled the Soviet Union with brutal control. Just days before Robeson's arrival, Stalin had plotted to assassinate his main political rival. Robeson heard about the execution of a number of counterrevolutionaries, and when asked for comment, he said, "It is the government's duty to put down any opposition to this really free society with a firm hand." The Soviet opposition to racism and fascism outweighed all other considerations for Robeson. He had gradually become more involved with politics, although he had never joined a political party in the United States. "He was an independent artist and would never submit to any kind of organizational discipline," recalled Paul Jr. in later years. Now, in the Soviet Union, Robeson was beginning to use his voice to express his views. This trip aroused in him "a new sense of purpose."

What touched him most was the Soviet attitude toward minorities, which was more tolerant than he had experienced before, even in England. Special theaters were available for collective farmers and various minority groups, who performed dramas in forty different languages. A state-sponsored Jewish Theatre was preparing a production of Shakespeare's *King Lear* in Yiddish. Robeson was amazed, given Russia's history of anti-Semitism under the rule of the Czars. At the Moscow Children's Theatre, he particularly enjoyed *The Negro Boy and the Monkey*, a popular play about an African child who comes to the Soviet Union to find his lost monkey. The theme delighted Robeson because it showed Soviet interest in Africa. Robeson and Essie were greatly impressed by their tours of the Theater School of the National Minorities, children's nurseries, and modern hospitals.

They saw no slums on their trip. Robeson said, "I made it a point to visit some of the workers' homes. . . . And I saw for myself. They all live in healthful surroundings." New apartment buildings were under construction in factory districts. During these years of the Great Depression in America and Western Europe, with millions of people out of work, the capitalist system seemed to have failed. Robeson and Essie believed that the Soviet Union's experiment created a better society. "This stuff about starvation [in Russia] is the bunk," he said in an interview. "Wherever I went I found plenty of food. Of course, it wasn't in every case the finest food, but it was healthful and everyone got enough to eat." Or so he thought.

They had come to Russia wearing heavy winter coats but weren't prepared for the extreme cold weather. When the temperature plunged to thirty-three degrees below zero, Essie went out and bought Robeson a warm, black, sable-lined coat. One snowy day as he was walking through a park in his coat, children spotted him and ran over to him. He spoke to them in Russian and they happily called him their "black Grandfather Frost." In Russian culture, Grandfather Frost, an old white man with a long white beard and floor-length fur coat, was the equivalent of Santa Claus. Robeson was touched by his new name and the fact that the children hadn't been taught to fear black men. He and Essie began to consider settling Paul Jr. in Russia for a few years. They thought he would enjoy "the sincere friendliness" of the Soviets toward people of color.

By the end of his visit, Robeson said to Eisenstein, "I feel like a human being for the first time since I grew up. Here I am not a Negro but a human being. Before I came I could hardly believe that such a thing could be. . . . Here, for the first time in my life I walk in full human dignity. You cannot imagine what that means to me as a Negro."

let my people go

chapter 17

— "Go Down, Moses"

Robeson returned to London full of enthusiasm for Soviet Russia. He even expressed a desire to live there someday. "Why, it's the only country in the world where I feel at home," he later said. However, he insisted that his interest was "non-political." Eisenstein's movie project was still in the discussion stage. Robeson was eager to start, but he didn't know that Eisenstein was waiting for official approval. The men had become close, and they corresponded, planning to work together on a number of films.

Robeson considered many other film offers and rejected most of them. He wanted to incorporate his new values into his work as an actor. One of his goals was to make a film on an African theme that would have a positive message. "Deep down inside me I am African," he said. He also wanted to earn enough money from movies and concerts to free him up financially and allow more time for meaningful projects and study.

In the spring of 1935, Robeson pursued his interests in portraying black culture truthfully, and reaching the working class. He planned to organize a repertory company that would produce plays with social themes. "When I step on to a stage in the future, I go on as a representative of the working–class," he said. "This isn't a bolt out of the blue. Not a case of a guy suddenly sitting down and deciding that he wants to join a workers' theatre. It began when I was a kid—a working-class kid living in that shack." He spoke about his experiences as a young man, "working in brick yards, in hotels, on docks and river boats."

For a start, Robeson joined a small group, the Arts Theater Club. In April, they put on a play titled *Basalik*, a story about a chief of an African country. They also performed *Stevedore*, a drama concerning black workers who organize against their white bosses and face down a lynch mob. Robeson took the lead and even sang in the show. Most of the black cast consisted of amateur actors, including Larry Brown. *Stevedore* closed quickly, though, and Robeson wasn't able to follow through on his plan to do the plays in the provinces.

In June, he and Brown went on a concert tour in Scotland, Ireland, and Wales. "I like singing for those audiences," he said. "There is sympathy between us—I sing better for them." In provincial towns, drivers would get off their trucks to shake his hand. Guys working on buildings shouted to him and told him they had his records. "I get on fine with those fellows," said Robeson. "We know each other. Those are the people I come from. And they understand what I sing."

"When I sing 'Let My People Go,'" explained Robeson, "I want it in the future to mean more than it has meant before. It must express the need for freedom not only of my own race . . . but of all the working-class."

Robeson scheduled the concerts a week apart to give him time for his studies. "All races all Peoples are not nearly as different from one from the other as textbooks would have it," he jotted down in his notebook. He felt passionate about learning the languages of folk songs from other countries and cultures. Only then, he thought, could he fully understand the meaning of the words and convey the spirit and emotions. Brown said, "After the greatest ovations, Paul would go home and read or study languages—an African dialect or Russian." He was even studying Chinese. Robeson had formed friendships with many West African and South African students, and people of color from the British colonies. He was also concentrating on learning Hebrew and sang "Avinu Malkeinu," a prayer recited during the Jewish High Holy Days of Rosh Hashanah and Yom Kippur.

Robeson said that Russian Jews were among his best friends in London and New York. "I think my people can take a lesson from the Jewish people in self-respect and pride in their culture." He asked a friend to teach him the Kaddish, a prayer recited in memory of the dead. While Robeson learned the Kaddish, he wore a yarmulke, a traditional skullcap worn by Jewish men, especially during prayer. "He chanted Yiddish rather well," said his friend, and Robeson later included the prayer in his concert programs. However, Robeson kept his main focus on African culture.

By now, Robeson hoped that Eisenstein would have gained permission to film their movie on Haiti, but his letters gave no sign of progress. Robeson decided to appear in a film version of *Show Boat*. He received an enormous salary of $40,000 ($720,692 in 2018 dollars), travel expenses for himself and Essie, and approval of location because he still refused to work in the segregated South. On September 25, 1935, he and Essie sailed for New York.

Before heading toward Hollywood, they stopped in Pittsfield, Massachusetts, to see Paul Jr. They had sent him there with Grandma Goode so that he could experience living in his own country. Paul Jr., almost eight, complained constantly. "I was tired of being away from my parents, tired of Grandma's inflexible tutelage," he recounted. He hated being "a black rich kid in an almost entirely white environment." Essie wrote him a letter and said, "We think the color is beautiful, and much more interesting than just plain uninteresting white." Despite her feelings, Paul Jr. was expelled from summer camp for fighting, and he ditched public school, refusing to go back.

The day after Robeson arrived in Pittsfield, he took Paul Jr. for a long walk in the woods. He listened to his son without interrupting, occasionally asking a question. When Paul Jr. was finished, Robeson looked down at him and said "in his soft, deep voice, 'When you come back to London next spring, you will live with Mama and me, and Grandma will live separately from us. I promise you.'"

Robeson and Essie aboard the
S.S. *Majestic* on their way to
New York to film the movie version
of *Show Boat*.

Grandma Goode (Mrs. Eslanda Goode)
and Paul Robeson, Jr., age seven,
February 15, 1935

In November, Robeson began shooting *Show Boat* at Universal. When he finished singing "Ol' Man River" with the orchestra and chorus, the musicians put down their instruments and applauded. Essie said, "They tell me it never happened before."

Robeson astonished the Universal sound engineers by revolutionizing the technique of "synching" a separate sound track with the visual track. He insisted on standing less than two feet from the microphone, closer than usual, and sang in an "intimate fashion" as he did for radio broadcasts rather than at full volume. While he was singing, he acted out the scene mentally, so the sound and the picture matched perfectly.

Robeson, as Joe, sings "Ol' Man River" in a scene from the motion picture production of *Show Boat*, 1936.

Show Boat opened at Radio City Music Hall in New York in January 1936. "Opulent spectacular," cheered critics. "Magnificent in scope." Once again, Robeson was deluged with film offers from top studios, but he turned them down. He was determined to do significant movies and plays about black people, and he even hoped to "experiment with comic roles."

He and Essie returned to England, so he and Brown could leave on another concert tour. When the tour ended in April, Robeson "made good on his promise" and brought Paul Jr. to live with them in the flat on Buckingham Street. Since Robeson spent a lot of time at home studying and writing, rehearsing music, and preparing roles, he could see his son often. "Paul's career dominated the household," wrote Paul Jr.

Paul Robeson and Lawrence Brown, in formal evening clothes, performing in a concert, 1936

Over the next few months, Robeson starred in a number of English films. *King Solomon's Mines* was set in Africa but was filmed in England. It featured a cast of twenty-seven thousand "natives," grass huts, and exploding volcanoes. Yet the movie, a "thundering good" epic adventure according to reviewers, disappointed Robeson.

However, *My Song Goes Forth*, a documentary on South Africa, delivered an important statement against the apartheid regime. A white minority owned nine-tenths of the land, completely controlled the government, and enforced segregation. Robeson called apartheid "South African Jim Crow." Black Africans who had moved to the cities to find work were forced to live in slums. Robeson had become friends with many African students and activists in London, and he strongly supported the struggle of anti-colonialists.

In a prologue for the documentary, Robeson wrote, "Africa was opened up by the white man for the benefit of himself—to obtain the wealth it contained." For the movie *Song of Freedom*, Robeson portayed a British dockworker who travels to Africa to find his roots. The film featured the song "Lonesome Road," which he recorded and performed in concerts:

> *Look down, look down*
> *That lonesome road*
> *Before you travel on.*

Shortly before Robeson left London to see filmmaker Sergei Eisenstein in the Soviet Union, he received a letter from the manager of the Old Vic Theatre Company. The company wanted him to star in a production of *Othello* after Christmas. Robeson refused saying he had already committed to a concert tour in the Soviet Union in the fall. But his real reason for turning down the offer was that he didn't feel ready to master the role. Robeson said, "Now was not the time."

Robeson visited Eisenstein and conducted more research on the conditions in both urban and rural areas outside Moscow. From his conversations with Eisenstein, and his own observations, Robeson gained a more realistic understanding of the Soviet environment under Stalin's rigid control. However, he never publicly expressed any criticisms of Stalin's Russia.

In the meantime, Essie and Paul Jr., traveled to South Africa, British East Africa, and Central Africa. For her, it was "one of those grand dreams come true." Old friends from Harlem and London who lived in Africa hosted the pair. She marveled at the beauty of Capetown but deplored the poverty and brutality she witnessed everywhere. Each day, she wrote in her diary about the gross injustices in South Africa, and later she used her notes for her book *African Journey*. She also took photographs. The experience of the trip to Africa transformed her into an anti-colonial writer and activist.

When Robeson returned to England, he starred in a film that showcased the problems of the working class. *Big Fella* told the story of a black dockworker, and Robeson pressured the scriptwriters to make the character a "steady, trustworthy sort of fellow." The movie included the song "My Curly Headed Baby," a lullaby that became a standard of Robeson's repertoire. He even learned how to sing it in Russian for a twelve-concert tour that he gave in the Soviet Union in October 1936, right after the film was finished. Soviet audiences responded to not only his singing, but also his fluent command of their language and his knowledge of Russian poetry and music.

Before starting the four-city tour, Robeson and Essie enrolled Paul Jr. in the best school in Moscow, attended by children of Soviet officials, including Stalin's daughter. Grandma Goode was visiting her sons in Moscow and agreed to stay on to help with Paul Jr. Robeson had promised his son he could live with him and Essie and seemed to be going back on his word. Evidently, they felt that school in Moscow would be better for their son while they traveled on tour.

Paul Jr. had just turned nine when he entered the equivalent of fifth grade, and he liked his classmates and teacher. Although he didn't know a word of Russian, he quickly learned the language. The American press reported the news that Paul Jr. was attending a Moscow school. A *Life* magazine photographer accompanied the Robesons on their trip to Moscow to enroll Paul Jr. and featured the story with a comment on Robeson's "Slav admiration."

A month later Robeson and Essie returned to Moscow to see how

Robeson and actors Henry Wilcoxon and Wallace Ford at the Pyramids near Cairo, during the filming of *Jericho* in 1937

their son was doing. This trip deepened Robeson's belief that the Soviet system of socialism was superior to the Western capitalist system. With Paul Jr. settled in Moscow under Grandma Goode's supervision, Robeson and Essie traveled to Egypt so he could begin work on a new movie, *Jericho*. Arriving in January 1937, Robeson set foot on the continent of Africa for the first time. "I want to be African," he said in an interview. "In my music, my plays, my films, I want to carry always this central idea: to be African."

The screenplay of his new film delighted him because the main character, Jericho Jackson, was a brave, intelligent, African American World War I soldier. He rescues dozens of men trapped below deck when a torpedo hits their troop ship off the coast of Algeria. Jericho accidentally kills an interfering sergeant and is unfairly sentenced to death. But he escapes and becomes the leader of a desert tribe—a "triumphant black hero." Robeson said, "It's the best part I have ever had for a picture."

To prepare for the role, he gathered information about Egypt, studied Egyptian history, viewed Egyptian movies, and even learned a little Arabic. During the month of shooting, he and Essie stayed just outside Cairo. "Cairo is a wonderful place," Robeson told an interviewer.

Essie was struck by the spectrum of skin colors. "It's great fun to see an enormously rich country like this, where the coloured folks are the bosses!" she wrote to friends.

Most of the filming took place in the desert near the pyramids. This was the actual spot where the Jews had been enslaved, in biblical times, by the Pharaoh and forced to make bricks and work in the fields. Moses had led his people out of this very desert and out of slavery. Robeson had been singing about this all these years with "Go Down, Moses." The words had recently taken on a new meaning to him, embracing the working class as well as people of his race.

On a day off, Robeson and a few others hired a guide and visited the Great Pyramid of Giza, climbing down a long passage to the King's Chamber. When the guide began describing the construction, one member of the group heard an echo and asked Robeson to sing. The first note "almost crumbled the place," recalled Robeson's costar Henry Wilcoxon. Robeson began to sing an aria from Mozart's opera *The Magic Flute* and the others were "spellbound—not moving, hardly breathing." As Robeson sang the last note, all of them "stood silently crying." Robeson cried too. "There were tears going down our faces," recalled Wilcoxon. No one spoke on the ride back to Cairo at sunset.

chapter 18

i must keep fighting until i'm dying

— "Ol' Man River" (as modified by Paul Robeson)

While Robeson was filming in Cairo, he followed the rising threat of fascism in Spain. The Spanish Civil War had started in July 1936. The Nationalists, led by General Francisco Franco, had rebelled against the democratically elected Republican government. Franco, with military support from Nazi Germany and fascist Italy, had taken control of the country. His ultimate goal was to be a dictator with unlimited power.

When Robeson returned to London after filming *Jericho*, he gave concerts and speeches to help Spain's Loyalists, who were fighting Franco. Robeson dedicated himself to what he described as the world's "greatest cause." He had found his political voice. Lowering his voice and speaking intensely, he warned about the dangers of fascism when others seemed to be ignoring the threat, or oblivious to it. Only the Soviet Union supported the Spanish Republic. "The cause of Spain is not only the concern of the Spanish people," he said. "We, as a people [Negroes], can no longer be indifferent to international events." To Robeson and many liberals, in Europe as well as the United States, the Spanish Civil War embodied a struggle between good and evil: democracy versus fascism.

April 26, 1937, was a market day in the Basque town of Guernica. People came from neighboring villages to buy and sell vegetables, chickens, and cattle. For three hours that day, the German air force, acting under orders from General Franco, bombed the town. People fled in panic. Hundreds were slaughtered.

Robeson responded to the Guernica massacre by singing and speaking at a huge rally for Spanish relief at London's Royal Albert Hall. "Fascism is no respecter of persons," Robeson said at the rally. "The blood-soaked streets of Guernica, that beautiful peaceful village nestled in the Basque hills, are proof of that. . . . The artist must take sides. He must elect to fight for freedom or slavery. I have made my choice. I had no alternative." His rousing speech was broadcast worldwide and immediately raised money. Volunteers from fifty-two countries had joined International Brigades to fight with the Loyalists. The American volunteers, known as the Abraham Lincoln Brigade, included many black men. Robeson also donated to help the families of black Americans fighting in Spain.

Robeson told Essie that he wanted to go to Spain and sing for the Loyalist troops. She asked why he would want to risk his life, his *voice*, in a war zone. He answered, "This is our fight, my fight. If fascism wins . . . the African, the Negro, the Jew go right to the bottom of the ladder." Essie decided to go with him. At first, the U.S. Department of State would not grant them visas, but finally, the Spanish embassy sent them "safe-conduct orders."

On Sunday, January 23, 1938, they arrived in Barcelona and learned that apartment buildings, schools, and hospitals had been hit in an air raid that morning. Journalists and photographers surrounded Robeson and took photos and notes. When asked why he had come to Spain, he said, "It is not only as an artist that I love the cause of democracy in Spain, but also as a Black. I belong to an oppressed race, discriminated against, one that could not live if fascism triumphed in the world."

A Spanish official provided Robeson and Essie with a car, an escort, and a driver, and they took off for Benicassim, a summer resort turned military base. Soldiers crowded the road, and one of them, a young black man, recognized Robeson and couldn't believe his eyes that the actor and singer was there. Robeson jumped out of the car and shook his hand. The soldier, one of the volunteers in the Abraham Lincoln Brigade, was from Harlem and had been fighting in Spain for eleven months.

General Francisco Franco in army uniform

A woman and child run for shelter in Spain
as an air-raid alarm sounds.

At an army hospital in Tarazona, Robeson sang outdoors without any accompaniment. "We then went thru the wards," recalled Essie, "Paul singing to the patients as we went. . . . All of them asked for Ol' Man River." Robeson had changed the closing lyrics to express his ideals:

I gets weary and sick of trying
I'm tired of living and scared of dying

were changed to

But I keep laughing instead of crying
I must keep fighting until I'm dying.

That night, they drove to Albacete, the headquarters of the International Brigade, volunteer soldiers from great Britain, Canada, and the United States. In the morning, at their training camp, fifteen hundred soldiers crowded into a church to hear Robeson sing, with no accompaniment. The men shouted requests for "Ol' Man River," "Water Boy," "Lonesome Road," and even the "Canoe Song" from the movie *Sanders of the River.* Robeson signed autographs, and Essie took messages to give to the solders' families.

Everywhere Robeson went, the troops recognized him. They had seen his movies, read about him, and heard his records; they were astounded he was actually there. A sergeant in the medical corps recalled that Robeson "lit up" the place. He was so "alive and vivid" that he was "like a magnet drawing you . . . in." After Robeson sang and talked with the men, they felt they had been with an old friend.

Robeson and Essie drove to Madrid for their next stop. The city had been bombed daily since 1936, and people were taking bets on "which windows would be broken by the raiding planes." The Robesons stayed at the Palace hotel, a mile and a half from the front line at Teruel. They could hear artillery and machine-gun fire, and the first two floors of the

Robeson surveys the wreckage in Madrid after the fascists bombed the city's apartment buildings.

hotel served as a hospital. From an observation tower, they saw trenches with government troops on one side and fascist rebels on the other. When a shell whizzed overhead and struck a building nearby, they took shelter in a staff room. A lieutenant and soldiers serenaded them with flamenco songs, and Robeson in turn sang first a Mexican folk song, "Encantadora Maria," in Spanish, and then spirituals. That night, Robeson broadcast from Madrid Central Radio Station and was heard throughout Spain as well as in England and America.

A day later, he sang to the Loyalist troops on the battlefield at Teruel, ensuring that loudspeakers were set up so the fascist rebels were forced to hear him too. Essie took photos of the Loyalist soldiers sitting at Robeson's feet, smiling and cheering. For one day, the war stopped as he sang the new lyrics of "Ol' Man River."

Robeson sings to the Loyalist troops at Teruel, Spain, 1938. The fascist rebels could also hear him through loudspeakers.

On January 29, he went to the barracks where the wounded were recuperating. A motion picture crew filmed him from every angle as he sang "Joshua," "Singin' with a Sword in My Hand," and "Fatherland," the rousing Soviet national anthem. He sang "Fatherland" in Russian, English, and Spanish. Soldiers propped themselves up in bed to listen and "went wild with joy."

When Robeson returned to London, he said that his trip to Spain had been "a turning point" in his life. "To me Spain is another homeland," he said, "because the people of this country are opposed to racial and class distinctions." In a note to himself, he wrote: "This is OUR STRUGGLE, and if we allow Republican Spain to suffer needlessly, we will ourselves suffer as deeply." Robeson realized that fascism had to be defeated in Spain or else it would spread worldwide.

arise, triumphant, the laboring folk

— "Border to Border," a popular Soviet song from the opera *Quiet Flows the Don*

Robeson linked the cause of Spain with oppressed people everywhere. The Western democracies, he felt, weren't doing enough to help the Loyalists. But he praised the Soviet Union for supporting the anti-fascist struggle.

Some people wondered if Robeson was secretly a communist since he was seen with friends who belonged to the Communist Party. Those who knew him said, "Robeson was not a joiner and had no time for meetings and studying Marxist texts." Another said, "Robeson was a free spirit and would not have functioned well within the [Communist] Party."

Robeson's London agent warned if he didn't cut back on speaking out about his political views, he might lose his concert bookings. "It is my duty as your representative," wrote his agent, "to point out that your value as an artist is bound to be very adversely affected. . . . You are doing yourself a great deal of harm."

Robeson ignored the advice and didn't seem to lose his popularity. When he and Brown gave a concert at Albert Hall in June 1938, the applause lasted so long when he walked onstage that Brown had to play a piano introduction twice, and Robeson gave a short speech thanking the audience before he could begin singing.

Robeson also defied his agent's warning by singing a popular Soviet song at a huge rally organized by the Emergency Peace Campaign (EPC), a movement that started in America and England and included student volunteers. Its goal was to avoid war and maintain peace. Robeson sang first in English, then in Russian:

> *From border unto border*
> *From ocean unto ocean*
> *Arise, triumphant, the laboring folk*
> *The brave Russian folk*
> *Yes, ready for sorrow*
> *Yes, ready to suffer*
> *Yes, ready to fight till death.*

Despite the efforts of the EPC and many others like Robeson, looming war still threatened. Hitler annexed Austria, and on March 14, 1938, triumphantly drove into Vienna. His plan was to to invade Czechoslovakia next. The Czech government appealed to England, France, and the Soviet Union for help, but these countries did nothing to stop Hitler's progress.

With increasing tensions in Europe, Robeson and Essie didn't want Paul Jr. and Grandma Goode to be trapped in the Soviet Union, even though they loved living there. At that time, reaching Moscow was difficult, except through German-controlled territory, and Robeson

Adolf Hitler, leader of the Nazi party, victoriously driving into Vienna in his six-wheeled car on March 14, 1938. Crowds of supporters cheer him and extend their arms in the Nazi salute.

remembered his horrifying experience in Berlin. In the face of imminent war, they sent for their son, who arrived in London. Grandma Goode returned to America.

This was a turning point for Robeson. He recognized the connection between international politics and the concerns of working-class people throughout the world. Robeson joined the Unity Theatre, "a people's theatre," sponsored by the British trade unions, and performed without pay. When asked why, he said, "I've managed to get some success, but there are thousands who haven't had the chance. It's not enough for one to be able to do it. I want everyone to have the chance." Robeson took the part of a union organizer in *Plant in the Sun*, a play about white and black workers going on strike. Since most members of the cast were actual carpenters and clerks who had daytime jobs, they held rehearsals at night and on weekends.

During the one-month run of the show, Robeson took time to appear at political rallies. At a reception held by the Indian League, he met and became friends with Jawaharlal Nehru, leader of the Indian National Congress, a group committed to breaking away from the British Empire and becoming independent. Nehru had been mentored by Mahatma ("great soul") Gandhi, an Indian lawyer who had been the leading figure in the Indian Home Rule Movement from 1916 to 1918. In 1929, leadership passed on to Nehru, while Gandhi took on a more spiritual role, fighting for his country's freedom with nonviolent methods, and protesting the oppression of India's poorest classes.

Nehru was westernized in his outlook and wanted good relationships with other countries. He went to see *Plant in the Sun*, and he and his sister had lunch with Robeson and Essie at their home. Paul Jr. remembered that to Nehru's amazement, Robeson recited some classic Hindu poetry in the original Hindi. Robeson pointed out the similarity in rhythm between Hindu and African American speech patterns. He and Nehru discussed how India might be governed when independence was won.

When *Plant in the Sun* closed, Robeson and Brown toured the

British provinces (Torquay, Swansea, and Eastbourne). More than ever, Robeson wanted to bring his music to working-class people. The duo performed "half"-concerts, three times a day, at movie palaces, charging reduced fees so that more people could afford to attend. No one of Robeson's stature had ever done that before. People who had low-paying jobs, and those on pensions or welfare, were able to hear Robeson sing in person. In Glasgow, Scotland, the crowd formed a line a quarter of a mile long outside the concert hall. Inside, Robeson "stood with tears in his eyes while the audience rose, clapped and shouted their appreciation of his work for Spain and oppressed humanity," reported the *Scotsman*. He started the varied program with "Water Boy" and "soon had everyone laughing with his rollicking rendition of 'Shortnin' Bread,'" a plantation song that was his son's favorite:

> *Put on the skillet, put on the lead*
> *Mammy's gonna bake a little shortnin' bread*
> *Mammy's little baby loves shortnin', shortnin'*
> *Mammy's little baby loves shortnin' bread.*

"It was the most successful tour we ever had," recalled Brown. "The people who formed the backbone of England—those who had kind hearts and were human—had always appreciated Paul. Now they seemed to love him more than ever because of what he was trying to do for the people."

After the tour ended, Robeson and Essie enrolled Paul Jr. in a London school for Soviet children. Paul Jr., almost eleven, had read about Stalin's purge trials, in which anyone he suspected of being disloyal was arrested and executed. Paul Jr. asked his father if the executions were justified. Robeson said that "dreadful things" had been done, that "innocent people had been sacrificed to punish the guilty," and that this was due to a situation in the Soviet Union that was "the equivalent of war." He said, "Gaining equality for the masses may require some temporary oppression and suppression of freedom" and "Russia was providing equality for all its citizens regardless of race or nationality."

As news spread about the purges, some people criticized Robeson for his sympathy with the Soviet Union. Even black ministers who were anti-Communistic accused Robeson of expressing communistic views. The director of the Associated Negro Press in Chicago wrote to Robeson and asked him if he was planning to make Russia his home. Robeson's American concert booking agent said, "The politics threatened his [Robeson's] business. . . . We argued about it quite a bit." But Robeson held firm in his views, and risked traveling down the "lonesome road."

Meanwhile, Hitler's anti-Jewish campaign intensified. On November 10, 1938, crowds of Germans roamed the streets, destroying Jewish shops and setting fire to synagogues. So many windows were smashed that the rampage was called *Kristallnacht* (Crystal Night). Nearly a hundred Jews were killed in twenty-four hours, and more than thirty thousand were arrested and sent to concentration camps. Few knew the horrors that would follow. President Franklin D. Roosevelt said, "I myself can scarcely believe that such things could occur in a twentieth-century civilization."

Now when Robeson sang "Go Down, Moses," it took on a new meaning. "It is no longer just a Negro song," he said. "In Germany, today, when the oppressed commit suicide, or try to escape unbearable conditions, their actions cry out against the terrorized land they wish to leave. Our *Moses*, with its 'let my people go,' never meant going to Heaven—the direction was really the North." Robeson explained that Sojourner Truth, a leader of the Abolitionist Movement to end slavery in America, had used the song when she passed through the woods to a Negro settlement. "And when the Negroes heard it, they knew it was a signal for a meeting," said Robeson. "When I sing, 'let my people go,' I can feel sympathetic vibrations from my audience, whatever its nationality."

Robeson maintained a hectic pace of political appearances for the causes dear to his heart. In December 1938, he attended the Welsh

The shattered storefront of a Jewish-owned shop in Berlin destroyed during Kristallnacht (the "Night of Broken Glass"). Jewish-owned stores were wrecked and looted all over Germany.

National Memorial Meeting at Mountain Ash in Wales to remember the Welsh men who had fought and died in the Spanish Civil War. He told the audience, "I am here because I know that these fellows fought not only for Spain but for me and the whole world." The Spanish Civil War had ended on March 28, 1939, when Madrid surrendered. Franco proclaimed victory three days later. The Loyalists had lost to the fascists, and more than 200,000 people were shot in mass executions. Millions were imprisoned.

When he spoke at the meeting in Wales, he met the president of the South Wales Miners' Federation, and the two had formed a bond. His next movie was *The Proud Valley*, about the miners, and met his standard of social significance. Later he said, "It was the one film I could be proud of having played in."

Robeson as David Goliath, with a fellow miner, in the movie *The Proud Valley*. The movie was shot in the Rhondda Valley of south Wales.

Shooting of the film began in August in the Welsh village of Maerdy. Robeson, age forty-one, had put on weight and had to slim down at a "nature-cure" rest home to prepare. During the filming, he and the other members of the cast lived with the villagers. Some of the locals appeared in the movie as supporting cast.

The story was based on an actual event. An American black

miner from West Virginia, David Goliath, went to Wales looking for work and became involved with the miners' struggle for a better life. In an opening scene, Robeson, as Goliath, hears the miners' choir singing and starts singing along with them. The choirmaster invites Goliath to join them. Soon Robeson winds up helping the poor miners with all their problems. When the choirmaster dies in a mining accident, Robeson sings the spiritual "Deep River" at the funeral:

> De-ee-ep river, my home is over Jordan
> Deep river, Lord, I want to cross over into campground.

While Robeson was shooting the movie, world events worsened. Germany and the Soviet Union signed a pact on August 23, 1939 agreeing that the two countries would not fight each other for ten years. In a public statement, Robeson said the pact in no way "weakened or changed" his beliefs or his sympathy with the Soviets. Privately, though, he feared the outbreak of war. His fears were realized on September 1, when Hitler's troops invaded Poland. Britain and France, honoring a treaty with Poland, declared war on Germany. World War II had begun.

Robeson and Essie quickly decided it was time to go home with Paul Jr. Having completed filming of *The Proud Valley* on September 25, Robeson was making a recording of "Deep River," while Essie was busy packing up their belongings. Robeson saw a rough cut of the film and was pleased. He said to reporters, "Having helped on many fronts, I feel that it is now time for me to return to the place of my origin."

who are you? america!

chapter 20

— "Ballad for Americans"

Robeson was in a "buoyant mood" when he and his family sailed into New York on October 12, 1939. As Paul Jr. recalled, "He and Essie had a bounce to their step when they walked off the gangplank." Robeson had "arrived home in the midst of a world crisis to offer leadership to his people." He said, "I feel closer to my country than ever."

Right away, Robeson spoke to the press. He condemned Hitler's Nazi Germany and Mussolini's fascist regime in Italy. He proclaimed himself an "anti-fascist, whether the struggle is in Spain, Germany, or here." But yes, he said, "the communists were his friends because they were strongly antiracist. Fascism, abroad *and* at home, was *the* enemy, not communism."

His lawyer, who greeted him at the dock, thought Robeson was "'going overboard' . . . politically." He also worried that Robeson might have lost his American audience after being away for twelve years. But Robeson remained confident.

Within a few weeks, Essie found an apartment for them in an elegant building at 555 Edgecombe Avenue on 160th Street in upper Harlem. Essie set up Paul Jr. and Grandma Goode in a penthouse above the apartment. Paul Jr. was enrolled in Ethical Culture Fieldston, a private school dedicated to social justice and racial equality.

Robeson visited old friends in Harlem and spent time with his brother Ben and sister-in-law Frances. Ben was now the pastor of the

Robeson uses his mighty voice to speak out for peace.

Mother A.M.E (African Methodist Episcopal) Zion Church on 137th Street. Robeson occasionally attended Sunday services there and sang hymns with the senior choir—"Balm in Gilead," "Steal Away," and "My Lord, What A Mornin'!" He also went to Philadelphia to see his older sister Marian.

Robeson was soon asked to appear on a CBS radio program, *The Pursuit of Happiness*, a salute to democracy to boost American spirit. The show featured a patriotic piece, "The Ballad of Uncle Sam," by Earl Robinson and John LaTouche. Robinson said of Robeson, "I have never had such a cooperative person to work with —*never*! There was nothing of the prima donna about him, nothing of arrogance." The ballad "reflected his [Robeson's] own great belief in what he thought was American democracy," said Brown. The producer renamed the piece "Ballad for Americans":

> *Man in white skin can never be free*
> *While his black brother is in slavery*
> *Our country's strong, our country's young*
> *And her greatest songs are still unsung.*

163

On Sunday, November 5, 1939, Robeson performed the eleven-minute work with an orchestra and chorus in a CBS studio. (He cupped his right hand over his ear as he sang, to hear himself better.) The opening of "Ballad" presented a brief history lesson about America's Founding Fathers. Then, as the chorus asked questions about both the leaders and ordinary workers who helped form the country, Robeson answered in speech and song. He sang of America's many religions and occupations. The chorus kept asking, "Who are you, Mister?"

Robeson responded,

> *You know who I am.*
> *For I have always believed it,*
> *And I believe it now,*
> *And you know who I am—AMERICA!*

The six hundred people in the studio audience stamped, cheered, and shouted for two minutes while the program was still on the air, and for fifteen minutes afterward. People called into CBS for hours, and hundreds of letters arrived. Producer Norman Corwin congratulated Robeson on "making radio history." Robeson repeated the broadcast on New Year's Day and recorded "Ballad for Americans" for Victor records.

Public demand led to another broadcast of the same program in the spring. Paul and Essie's friend, Marie Seton, was visiting New York and was staying at a hotel around the corner from the CBS studio. She invited Robeson and Essie to have lunch with her after the program. They went to her room and started catching up. Shortly after, the hotel manager called and said to Seton, "If you and Mr. and Mrs. Robeson are planning to have lunch, our restaurant will refuse to serve you. Our patrons would object to Mr. and Mrs. Robeson in this restaurant." Seton was outraged. "I thought of the wildly applauding crowd at the C.B.S. studio," she recalled, "and of the writers, actors and intellectuals living in the hotel who paid tribute to Paul Robeson as an artist." As if he could read her thoughts, Robeson said, "Can we get something to eat sent up here? I don't eat in hotel restaurants here—outside of Harlem."

Although he was the spokesman for the All-American ballad, and world famous, he was still treated like a second-class citizen in the United States. But not in Russia. Robeson's commitment to the Soviet Union grew despite news of Stalin's purges and persecution of the peasants. Then, on November 30, 1939, Soviet troops invaded Finland. Stalin wanted to occupy Finland and turn it into a Soviet republic attached to Russia. Most people were stunned and supported the Finns, but Robeson claimed that the Soviet Union was conducting a "defensive war" to protect its borders. He turned down an invitation to sing at a benefit for "brave little Finland." Robeson's concert booking agent was worried. He said, "If it gets around that Paul is endorsing Stalin against the Finns he can kiss his concert tour goodbye."

Yet Robeson's popularity with the public remained high. In a revival of *Show Boat* with the Los Angeles Civic Light Opera Association, the opening-night crowd gave Robeson a standing ovation as soon as he appeared. Robeson and Brown performed "Ballad for Americans" at the Hollywood Bowl for 30,000 fans. The sold-out crowd was estimated to be the largest for any event at the Bowl. But Robeson had trouble finding a good hotel room. His agent tried to book him into the Beverly Wilshire, a luxury hotel whose guests had included U.S. presidents and movie stars. The hotel finally agreed to give Robeson a hundred-dollar-a-day suite on the condition that he use an assumed name and take meals in his room. Robeson agreed, because he knew he'd be recognized anyway. But, in protest, he sat in the lobby of the hotel for two hours every afternoon. When asked why he bothered, Robeson replied, "To ensure that, the next time black singers and actors come through, they'll have a place to stay."

Upon Robeson's return to New York, Essie announced that she wanted to buy a house in Enfield, Connecticut, a large, colonial-style house, complete with a pool, servants' quarters, and a separate recreation building that included a bowling alley. Before closing the deal, Essie asked the bank to receive assurances from neighbors in Enfield that they would not object to a black family moving into their white community. The sale went through, but the big house needed fixing up. One of the repairmen said of Robeson, "He's gonna hafta sing alotta songs to heat this place."

In June 1941, Essie, Paul Jr., and Grandma Goode moved to Connecticut. "We are all simply crazy about the country," Essie wrote to friends. "Big Paul loves the quiet and low gear of the place, and flies home for every moment he can spare even when on tour."

Paul Jr. entered high school in Enfield. "I experienced no racism there," he recalled. "I remember the first school dance I went to; one of the most popular girls in school walked all across the floor to ask me to dance, to break the ice." And Paul Jr. played football on the school's team, just like his dad. Robeson occasionally spent time at the high school. At the annual Class Night, he showed up unannounced and sang four songs. But he really preferred New York and stayed with friends in their Greenwich Village townhouses whenever he was in the city.

Not long after the Robesons moved to Connecticut, German troops invaded the Soviet Union. The Russians allied with Britain and France, and suddenly the Soviet Union was a heroic nation battling fascism. Robeson intensified his efforts to support the Soviets and raise money for aid. He hoped that President Roosevelt would soon join the allies in the war against Germany.

Six months later, the Japanese attacked Pearl Harbor, and the United States entered World War II. Robeson worked diligently for the war effort, selling war bonds, participating in rallies, and singing for the troops at the USO (United Service Organizations) centers, which had been founded to provide entertainment for the U.S. Armed Forces and their families. The director of the CIO (Congress of Industrial Organizations) Servicemen's Center in San Francisco wrote to Robeson and said, "I can tell you that an awfully large number of boys are looking forward to your coming. Every night they've been asking us 'if its really true you're coming.'"

Robeson traveled across the country appearing in concerts, at dinners, and at meetings, speaking out about defeating fascism and combating oppression at home. "His strategy was to connect the war against fascism with the black freedom struggle," wrote Paul Jr. In his speeches, Robeson warned that discrimination against black voters in the South, and segregation in the Armed Forces, were arousing "the bitterest resentment among black Americans."

Unbeknownst to Robeson, FBI Director J. Edgar Hoover had assigned agents to follow his activities and monitor his mail and phone calls. Hoover was obsessively opposed to the labor movement and Communism. He kept secret files on political radicals, and illegally wiretapped people suspected of subversive activity. He considered Communism "the most evil, monstrous conspiracy against man since time began." In a meeting with President Roosevelt, he declared that the West Coast longshoremen's union "was practically controlled by

J. Edgar Hoover, the first director of the Federal Bureau of Investigation, sits at his desk talking on the phone. He had total control of the FBI and could promote or fire any agent without giving a reason.

Communists" and that the United Mine Workers of America had "strong Communist leanings." These were just some of the unions that Robeson supported.

Hoover was racist, too. He had grown up in Washington, DC, then a segregated city. When he became Director of the FBI, he hired only a few black people. One of the black "agents" was his chauffeur, and another was an elevator operator. Instead of investigating racist organizations like the Ku Klux Klan, he harassed black leaders.

As early as January 1941, Hoover's special agents were reporting to FBI headquarters that Robeson was "reputedly a member of the Communist Party." A U.S. immigration inspector based in Vancouver wrote that Robeson had been visited by representatives of the Civil Liberties League and the local Housewives League, which included "in its membership the wives of well known communists." In February, the FBI started a file, number 100-12304, on Paul Robeson, Sr. The first page referred to a letter, received by the Seattle Office, "with reference to PAUL ROBESON, prominent American Negro vocalist, and alleged member of the Communist Party."

In the spring of 1941, the Dies Committee of the House of Representatives held hearings on "un-American activities." Hoover sent agents to spy on the committee and its findings. At the hearings, a research director, J.B. Matthews cited an interview with Robeson five years earlier that was published in a book titled *Soviet Russia Today*. The report came back to Hoover, which he felt was "proof" that Robeson had "made his choice for communism."

The FBI began to tap Robeson's phone and "bug" apartments where he was staying. Another letter from an agent, dated March 18, 1942, reported on Robeson's supposed connections with the Communist Party, based on the fact that he was due to appear at a dinner for the Joint Anti-Fascist Refugee Committee. The agent wrote that the real purpose of the fundraiser was to help transport communists to Mexico and Latin American countries.

Ⅎederal Bureau of Inuestig

United States Department of Justice

Seattle, Washington

February 17, 1941

Director
Federal Bureau of Investigation
Washington, D. C.

Dear Sir: RE: PAUL ROBESON;
                      INTERNAL SECURITY - R.

        There are enclosed herewith for the information of the
Bureau and with copy of this letter to the New York Division,
copies of a letter dated at Seattle, Washington, January 16,
1941 received by the Seattle Office from the District Director,
United States Immigration and Naturalization Service at Seattle,
with reference to PAUL ROBESON, prominent American Negro
vocalist, and alleged member of the Communist Party.

                   Very truly yours,

                   A. CORNELIUS, JR.,
                   Special Agent in Charge

EEB:MC

cc New York City
Enc.

ENCL 6

CONTAINED
111 701 80

RECORDED
&
INDEXED

100-304-1

FEDERAL BUREAU OF INVESTIGATION
6   FEB 19 19
U.S. DEPARTMENT OF JUSTICE

2

The cover of Paul Robeson's FBI File, 100-12304, and the first item in it, a letter from Special
Agent A. Cornelius, Jr., dated February 17, 1941. Eventually, thousands of reports were added to
the file, which is now available for viewing online.

An agent was present in August 1942 when Robeson visited Camp Wo-Chi-Ca (Workers' Children's Camp). The interracial camp, located in New Jersey, was sponsored by the International Workers Order, a communist group. Robeson had first visited Wo-Chi-Ca in 1940 and returned every year, to sing, play ball, and talk to the campers. In a file marked "Confidential," the agent noted that two hundred and sixty of the children had parents who were members of the Communist Party.

The FBI desperately wanted to prove that Robeson was a spy. They knew that he was studying Chinese songs of resistance to the Japanese occupation. Japan had invaded China in 1937, and in 1940, the country entered an alliance with fascist Germany and Italy. The Secretary of the Shanghai YMCA met Robeson in New York and coached him in both the Chinese language and the musical style required for performing the songs, which Robeson began singing at benefits for China. Once, he accidentally left a notebook containing Chinese characters in a taxi. An FBI agent who had been trailing him found it and eagerly forwarded it to FBI headquarters. The FBI Translation Section pored through the notebook, but even Hoover realized it did not contain a secret code. Yet he redoubled his efforts to brand Robeson a member of the Communist Party. Robeson's file kept growing until it eventually contained thousands of documents and became the largest file in the FBI.

the right to speak my mind

— "The House I Live In"

Throughout 1942, as Allied troops stormed against the enemies in Europe, Asia, and the South Pacific, Robeson used his voice to fight for democracy. He paid tribute to the chief Allied powers—the United States, Great Britain, the Soviet Union, and China—in the song "The Four Rivers." The lyrics expressed his hopes for world harmony:

> *Here's the story of the four rivers*
> *That the eyes of the world are on*
> *They're called the Thames, the Mississippi*
> *And the Yangtze, and the Don*
> *Oh, the four rivers*
> *Apart as they can be*
> *But they discovered how to get together*
> *Where the rivers roll to the sea.*

During a cross-country concert tour, he stopped to record radio broadcasts in response to a request from President Roosevelt and the secretary of war. Robeson broadcast songs that would inspire international resistance to the major countries the U.S. and its allies were fighting—Germany, Italy, and Japan, the Axis powers. He sang to the Red Army troops in Russian, to the Chinese troops in Chinese, and to the underground movement in Germany in German. He even learned a Norwegian song for the resistance in Nazi-occupied Norway.

Many black people protested having to serve in a war against fascism while Jim Crow racism persisted throughout the United States. Even the United States military was segregated. Yet some black men and women enlisted in the face of racial discrimination. Black service personnel had their own units, barracks, and mess halls. Robeson violated his principle of not performing for segregated audiences by adding appearances at military bases to his regular concert schedule. After performances, he would hang out in the black canteen. As Robeson stepped up his activities on behalf of the Allies, Hoover stepped up surveillance of him.

When Robeson returned home to Enfield during a break in his cross-country tour, he and Margaret Webster, an actress and director, began planning to present *Othello* in New York. At age forty-four, Robeson felt ready to play the part of the Moor of Venice in Shakespeare's tragedy. Webster said, "I believed that a production of the play with him in it could be a landmark in the American theatre and in the history of American social consciousness." But when she contacted producers, she wrote that "everyone was scared," to mount a play in which a black man loves and kills a white woman. She and Robeson decided to produce the play themselves and try it out in summer stock (regional summer theaters that featured Broadway stars).

The Brattle Theatre in Cambridge, Massachusetts, and the McCarter Theatre in Princeton, New Jersey, agreed to let them put on the play in the summer of 1942.

Webster chose a talented young couple, Uta Hagen and her husband José Ferrer, to play the roles of Desdemona and Iago. The cast had only two weeks to rehearse before opening at the Brattle. They worked ten hours a day. "Robeson is going to be *very* bad," Hagen wrote to her father, "but he's an angel."

Robeson as Othello in the Broadway production
at the Shubert Theatre, 1943

Robeson, as Othello, has just killed Desdemona,
played by actress Uta Hagen in the Broadway
production.

Webster wrote that Robeson had "no technique" and depended on his intelligence and energy. She said, "Fortunately his tremendous vocal resources protect him." The play opened in the first week of August during an intense heat wave and sold out immediately. It was so hot that Robeson had to wring out his robes between scenes, but the performance was a success. Harvard undergrads pounded their heels and clapped their hands. Shouts of "Bravo!" accompanied the many curtain calls. A reporter marveled that "the staid old walls didn't burst from the noise and enthusiasm." Finally, the entire company joined the audience in singing the national anthem.

Reviews the next day were glowing. "A great artistic achievement," wrote a Boston critic. *The New York Times* praised Robeson's "heroic and convincing" performance. *Variety* declared that "no white man should ever dare presume" to play the role again. Producers swamped Webster with offers to present the play in New York. She finally selected the Theatre Guild.

The show had to be postponed until October 1943 because Webster and Robeson had prior commitments. Robeson completed the two-week run of *Othello* at the McCarter in Princeton, his hometown. Albert Einstein, the brilliant scientist and a resident of Princeton, saw the play and came backstage to congratulate Robeson. Einstein had fled to the United States from Nazi Germany in 1933, and he worked at the Institute for Advanced Study in Princeton. In 1935, he had heard Robeson sing spirituals at the McCarter Theatre and went back stage then as well. The two men struck up a friendship as they discussed world affairs and "discovered that they shared not only a passion for music, but a hatred of fascism." Now, in 1942, Einstein urged Robeson to take *Othello* on a national tour after its Broadway run.

As soon as the play closed at the McCarter, Robeson left for a hectic schedule of concerts and political appearances. In Manhattan, he spoke at a mass rally in support of the Free India movement. Like his friend Nehru, he believed that colonialism had to be ended. Robeson told the crowd that the war against the Axis powers was "a war for the liberation of all peoples, all races, all colors oppressed anywhere in the world."

FBI agents tracked his moves and reported that "the Communists" had met at the rally. The bureau described Robeson as a communist functionary. "His activities in behalf of the Communist Party are too numerous to be recorded."

Robeson continued his schedule of appearances, speaking and singing to thousands of aircraft workers, and troops at military camps. After seventy performances from Idaho to New Hampshire, Robeson returned home to Enfield to rest and be with his family. He and Paul Jr. became closer. They played ping-pong and chess and talked. "My father was interested in what I thought and felt," wrote Paul Jr. "He shared more stories about his past than ever before."

Robeson makes a speech at Madison Square Garden in New York in the 1940s.

At fifteen, Paul Jr. was about to enter his senior year of high school. At sixteen, he would be eligible for a driver's license. Robeson warned him of the dangers. "You'll be a target of the state police," he said, "especially after dark." Robeson knew that because his son was African American, he would be at risk from assault by the police. He urged Paul Jr. to stay alert whenever he found himself in an unfamiliar white neighborhood. "Always be conscious of where you are, what is going on, and who is around you."

Politics was also a topic of discussion. Paul Jr., who had joined a left-wing youth group and was thinking about joining the Communist Party, asked Robeson why he had never joined. Robeson replied that he didn't want to submit himself to Party discipline. "I do what I want to, say what I want to, sing what I want to. I listen to what others say, but I make my own decisions."

Over the summer of 1943, Robeson prepared for *Othello*. He worked out with a trainer, lost weight, and grew a goatee for the role. Just before rehearsals were to start, the Theatre Guild decided to replace Uta Hagen and José Ferrer. Ferrer's draft status was uncertain, so he could be called up for military service at any time. Robeson argued that he worked well with the couple and wouldn't continue in the play unless the Ferrers were rehired. They reached an agreement and the Ferrers stayed on.

During the six-week rehearsal period that Robeson had insisted on, he expressed doubts about his acting to Hagen. "I don't have it," he confided, as he tried to dig to the bottom of his character. He regretted that he had never had training as an actor. "Directors assumed that I knew what I was doing," he said, "when the fact was that I had no technique at all." Webster told him to "just look at what Shakespeare *says*." Robeson did and told an interviewer, "I took *Othello* apart bit by bit to find out what each word meant." He portrayed the character as "a great Negro warrior" and said, "I played it my way. I am not a great actor like José Ferrer. . . . All I do is feel the part. I made myself believe I am Othello, and I acted as he would act."

One of his biggest problems was expressing rage on demand. He had been brought up to keep his anger in check, although he knew what it was like to be "out of my head" with fury. To bring that emotion to the stage, he remembered the time at Rutgers when he had tried out for the football team and one of the players had stomped on his hand and torn out his fingernails. It worked. Another challenge he faced was to bring his voice down. He said he was "constantly careful not to make my lines too musical, not to sing my lines, but to SPEAK them MUSICALLY."

The play previewed in New Haven on September 11, 1943, and Robeson invited his whole family to attend. Ben and Frances drove up from Harlem with their three daughters. Robeson's sister Marian and her husband and daughter came in from Philadelphia. Of course, Essie, Paul Jr., and Grandma Goode were there too. "The performance was a hit with both audience and critics," wrote Paul Jr. A few days later, Essie sent Robeson a letter: "The family loved the play and were seething with pride over your performance. I love you, Mr. Robeson."

On the evening of October 19, 1943, *Othello* opened at the Shubert Theatre. Webster wrote, "I have never been so paralytic with fright. For the first time in the United States a Negro was playing one of the greatest parts ever written." In the final lines of the play, Robeson spoke Shakespeare's words with moving solemnity:

I pray you, in your letters,
When you shall these unlucky deeds relate,
Speak of me as I am; nothing extenuate,
Nor set down aught in malice.
Then must you speak of one
That loved not wisely but too well . . .

I kissed thee ere I killed thee.
No way but this, killing myself,
To die upon a kiss.

As Robeson delivered these words, two young girls in the audience sat entranced. One of them, Ellen Popper, recalled wishing they could tell "the tormented Moor that he had been betrayed." Her friend's father had been Robeson's classmate at Rutgers, and Robeson invited the girls to sit in a box with access to backstage. "The final moment, when Mr. Robeson stood in his magnificent orange-red robe and projected his torment to all of us, was almost too much to bear," remembered Ellen. "We cried for him and midst our tears and the applause the curtain descended."

As soon as the curtain fell, the girls hurried down the stairwell. "Breathlessly (still hearing the applause out front), we rushed up to Mr. Robeson, whose skin glistened with perspiration from the emotion he had expended." The girls asked him for his autograph. "Then this beautiful man smiled the broadest grin I think I have ever seen," wrote Ellen, "took both of us by the hand and as the curtain rose for another curtain call, we found ourselves facing the audience, our small hands clasped in those large enveloping ones." Later, she wondered what the audience must have thought when they saw "that huge gentle black actor taking his bows while holding the hands of two little blond-headed girls in white gloves and Mary Jane shoes."

After ten curtain calls, Robeson and Webster had to make speeches to end the evening. Webster turned to Robeson, who was surrounded by the cast, and said, "Paul, we are all very proud of you tonight." The next morning, Robeson read the reviews with his friends. The *World-Telegram* hailed this *Othello* as "one of the most memorable events in the history of the theater." One of his friends recalled that "Paul began to beam and look very pleased." Robeson turned to her and said, "Boy I'm lucky. Did you ever know such luck as I have?"

scandalize my name

chapter 22

— "Scandalize My Name"

One of the few people unimpressed by Robeson's triumph in *Othello* was J. Edgar Hoover. After receiving reports from his agents about Robeson's speeches at political events, and his recording of the new Soviet National Anthem, Hoover believed that Robeson was "undoubtedly 100% Communist." Hoover recommended that Robeson be considered for immediate arrest in the event of a national emergency. On April 30, 1943, a card marked "custodial detention" was issued for Robeson. By August, he was labeled "a leading figure in the Communist party . . . actively attempting to influence the Negroes of America to Communism."

Robeson seemed unaware of the FBI's surveillance and continued to speak out for his favorite causes: obtaining equal rights for African Americans, winning freedom for people under colonial rule, helping the workers' unions, and promoting support for the Soviet Union. Hoover branded these causes as "activities in behalf of the Communist Party." FBI agents trailed Robeson and illegally tapped his phone conversations. The more Robeson expressed his views, the more Hoover devoted personal attention to his file. To the FBI, Robeson was classified as a dangerous subversive in the category of a spy.

Robeson gave Hoover ample opportunity to malign him. On December 3, 1943, he spoke at a meeting with the owners of major league baseball teams to discuss black players being barred from playing professional baseball. "I come here as an American and former athlete."

Then he cited his own experiences in college football, which had never resulted in a racial disturbance. "The time has come that you must change your attitude toward Negroes," he said. When Robeson finished speaking, the club owners applauded. Although nothing changed that season, they had listened and unanimously agreed to remove barriers preventing the signing of black baseball players.

On April 16, 1944, the Council on African Affairs (CAA) sponsored a huge celebration for Robeson's forty-sixth birthday. Robeson had cofounded the CAA in London back in the 1930s. It was a left-wing group dedicated to winning freedom for colonies in Africa and independence for India. Robeson had continued to support the CAA and was the chairman. It was the first organization that connected the struggle of African Americans for civil rights and the fight of colonized people in Africa and Asia for freedom. Eight thousand people gathered at New York City's Armory for the event, and thousands were turned away. Mary McLeod Bethune, a black civil rights activist and educator, hailed Robeson as "the tallest tree in our forest." As Robeson responded to the tributes, he choked up and grew teary. "Save your voice, Paul!" yelled someone in the audience. The crowd joined an all-black soldiers' chorus, singing "Happy Birthday, Dear Paul." Army intelligence agents were also at the Armory that day and shared a detailed report with the FBI.

Agents began to follow Essie, too, a political and social activist in her own right. On June 10, 1944, Hoover sent a letter to the special agent in New Haven. He wrote that a "security index card has been prepared at the Bureau." The card labeled Essie a communist. Like Paul, she belonged to the CAA, and she participated in various public programs. Recently, she had attended an interracial meeting of influential women in Georgia. The state's segregationist laws made the meeting illegal, but Essie and the other women still dared to gather. Essie also published her book, *African Journey*, which established her as an expert on Africa and a recognized lecturer.

Without realizing that he and Essie were at risk, Robeson carried on with his political and theatrical life. *Othello* closed in July 1944, after 296 performances. The show set a Broadway record for a Shakespearean production. In September, the cast began a nine-month coast-to-coast tour of the United States and Canada.

On the tour, Robeson insisted that they perform only in theaters that were not segregated, setting an important precedent. Their last stop was Chicago. During the run, news came that President Franklin D. Roosevelt had died suddenly on April 12, 1945. That night, the cast dedicated their performance to the president's memory. At the curtain call, Robeson praised the president as a person who had believed that the "rights of man [were] more important than the rights of private property." Robeson predicted that Roosevelt's death would change things, and not for the better.

On May 8, 1945, V-E Day, the Germans surrendered to the Allies, ending the war in Europe. But Japanese military leaders refused to surrender unconditionally. Roosevelt's successor, President Harry S. Truman, decided to use the atomic bomb against Japan. On August 6, American pilots dropped the bomb on the city of Hiroshima. Hundreds of thousands of people were killed, mostly civilians. Houses were obliterated. Still, the Japanese generals would not back down. On August 9, a second atomic bomb was dropped on the city of Nagasaki. Finally, on August 15, the Japanese surrendered. World War II was over.

That month, Robeson and Brown traveled overseas on a concert tour sponsored by the USO. They were accompanied by white musicians, forming the first interracial unit sent to entertain the troops. During the month-long tour, they gave thirty-two performances, including a concert at Hitler's opera house in Nuremberg, Germany. At a German army base, Robeson spoke with soldiers who had liberated the concentration camps. He listened intently as they described the shocking horrors they had seen—thousands of unburied dead bodies, walking skeletons too sick and starved to survive being free. Robeson's appearances "inspired

Nagasaki, Japan, under atomic bomb attack by the U.S. Army on August 9, 1945. The bomb known as "Fat Man" killed between 40,000 and 75,000 people immediately, while 60,000 others suffered severe injuries.

Robeson talks to African American soldiers during his concert tour to entertain the troops in France, Czechoslovakia (now the Czech Republic), and Germany, August 1945.

black soldiers throughout Europe and gave a badly needed boost to their morale," wrote Paul Jr. A white serviceman in Germany described his experience when he heard Robeson sing the revised closing lines of "Ol' Man River":

> I'se so weary and almost dyin'
> But I keeps laffin' and keeps on tryin'.

"As he sang those words, his face lit up in a ferocious fighting grin, and he pounded his fist in his hand and sang directly at the group of colored boys in the audience," wrote the serviceman. "And you can bet that I was saying with every atom of me, 'More and more power to you.'"

Back home, Robeson received the NAACP's Springarn Medal, the most prestigious award in the black community. The medal is given annually "to the man or woman of African descent and American citizenship, who shall have made the highest achievement during the preceding year or years in any honorable field of human endeavor."

Upon receiving the award at the banquet, Robeson stunned the audience with his speech, which criticized America for resisting civil rights reform. He pointed out that black soldiers returning to America no longer wanted to be treated like second-class citizens. After proudly serving their country, they expected changes at home but instead encountered an outbreak of racial violence aimed at "uppity" black veterans. He cited Mississippi, where racism was especially strong, and black veterans were prevented from registering to vote by literacy tests, property tax receipts, and terrorist threats. White supremacists, he noted, enforced these unjust obstacles so that black citizens couldn't exercise their political rights. And they weren't about to stop.

Robeson also attacked the government for showing renewed signs of hostility toward Russia. "Full employment in Russia is a fact, and not a myth," he said, "and discrimination is non-existent." Lastly, he lashed out against America's support of colonialism, and emphasized India's continued struggle for independence. FBI agents reported his every word.

In September, Robeson and Brown left on the longest concert tour they had ever made, which continued into the spring of 1946. Along the way, Robeson was appalled by the wretched housing conditions and poor job opportunities he witnessed in the black community. He heard reports of police brutality and an increase in the number of lynchings. Brown said that Robeson was in a "foul mood" for most of the tour and "more difficult to work with than during all the years before. . . . He constantly felt he could not sing another concert." Yet Robeson was at the peak of his power as a singer and still a great favorite with audiences.

More and more, Robeson concerned himself with the horrific attacks on black Americans. Between June 1945 and September 1946, fifty-six black people were brutally lynched. In South Carolina, Sergeant Isaac, Woodard Jr., a decorated African American veteran who had served in the South Pacific for fifteen months, was falsely arrested and then blinded in a vicious beating by a white police chief who was later tried and acquitted. The NAACP had tried without success to convince President Roosevelt to support a federal anti-lynching bill. On September 12, Robeson spoke with indignation at a rally at Madison Square Garden. *"Stop the lynchers!"* he cried. "What about it, President Truman? Why have you failed to speak out against this evil?"

Robeson and black leader W. E. B. Du Bois planned a conference in Washington, DC, to launch "an American crusade against lynching." Albert Einstein agreed to cochair the project. The conference took place on September 23, with 1,500 black and white attendees, representing various organizations.

Robeson headed a delegation that went to the Oval Office to meet President Truman. But when the president was asked to issue a public statement denouncing lynching, he said the time wasn't right for him to speak out. Robeson pointed out that in Nuremberg, Germany, prosecutors from the Allied nations were presenting cases against Nazis accused of war crimes against humanity. He said it seemed "inept" for the United States government to take the lead in prosecuting Nazis while failing to "give justice to Negroes in this country." Robeson warned that the mood of black people was changing. He told Truman that if the federal government refused to defend them against murder, blacks would have to defend themselves. Truman angrily shook his fist at Robeson and said that sounded like "a threat." Robeson assured him it was not a threat but rather a statement of fact. Truman abruptly ended the meeting.

Later that day, Robeson stood in front of the Lincoln Memorial and gave a radio address. "People of America," he said, "we appeal to you to help wipe out this inhuman bestiality, this Ku Klux Klan hooded violence." He said he felt ashamed that so many years after President Abraham Lincoln's Emancipation Proclamation freeing enslaved people, in 1863, it was still necessary to speak "of the lynch terror and mob assaults against Negro Americans."

Robeson marches at a civil rights protest in Washington, DC, 1948.

Two weeks later, Robeson was called to testify before the Joint Fact-Finding Committee on Un-American Activities in California. The committee was formed to investigate people deemed subversive. The chairman began by asking Robeson about his trips to the Soviet Union. He asked if Robeson's son had been educated in the Soviet Union, and if he was a citizen of the Soviet Union. "He is not," replied Robeson. "He was born in the United States."

Then the chairman asked Robeson if he was a member of the Communist Party and added, "I ask it of everybody, so don't feel embarrassed." Robeson said, "No. I am not embarrassed. . . . Every reporter has asked me that. . . . Only you might ask me if I am a member of the Republican or Democratic Party. As far as I know, the Communist Party is a very legal one in the United States. . . . If I wanted to join any party, I could just as conceivably join the Communist Party, more so today than I could join the Republican or Democratic Party. But I am not a Communist."

as soon as ever my back was turned

chapter 23

—"Scandalize My Name"

Robeson loved the song "Joe Hill." Joe Hill was a Swedish–American laborer and union organizer in Utah, who had been convicted of murder without conclusive evidence and executed at the Sugar House Prison. Robeson and workers everywhere regarded him as a martyr. In March 1947, Robeson gave a concert at the University of Utah in Salt Lake City, near the prison where Joe Hill died. He closed with the ballad:

> I dreamed I saw Joe Hill last night
> Alive as you or me
> Says I, but Joe, you're ten years dead
> I never died, says he
> I never died, says he.

When Robeson finished singing, he told the audience, "You've heard my final concert for at least two years, and perhaps for many more. I'm retiring here and now from concert work—I shall sing, from now on, for my trade union and college friends; in other words, only at gatherings where I can sing what I please."

Robeson had become an honorary member of several unions that belonged to the Congress of Industrial Organizations (CIO), a group made up of unions that organized workers in mass-production industries, such as auto manufacturing. Robeson backed the CIO because they welcomed black workers and allowed communists to participate as union leaders. At one of his speeches, Robeson declared, "The best way my race can win justice is by sticking together in progressive labor unions." He joined picket lines of striking workers and made regular appearances at union conventions and rallies.

Robeson still had commitments to fulfill. But when he arrived in Peoria, Illinois, his concert was cancelled because the House Un-American Activities Committee (HUAC) had included his name on a list of people who supported the Communist Party. The congressional committee had been established to investigate "disloyal" activities of fascists and communists in the United States, especially people in the arts. The mayor of Peoria called off a reception for Robeson and denied him a place to sing. Then, the Board of Education in Albany, New York, cancelled a concert he was scheduled to give at a high school. Black sponsors of the event sued the board, and eventually a state judge ruled that Robeson could perform as long as he made no political statements during the concert.

J. Edgar Hoover stepped up the FBI's attacks on Robeson. Surveillance intensified. Although Hoover had no proof that Robeson was a communist, he urged his media contacts to vilify Robeson in the press. Paul Jr. wrote that his father "remained outwardly unconcerned." Yet Robeson once said to reporters, "I have been all over the world and the only time I have seen hysteria reach these heights was in Spain under Franco and Germany under Hitler."

Robeson took a greater risk when he decided to support Henry Wallace for president in the election of 1948. Wallace had been vice president under President Roosevelt, until he was replaced by Harry Truman. Wallace and like-minded citizens formed the Progressive Party. Wallace accepted support from union workers, liberals, and even communists, while other members of the Progressive Party rejected communist backing. Wallace said that he found "nothing criminal in the advocacy of different economic and social ideas."

Robeson and Lawrence Brown performing at Albany's Philip Livingston Junior High School on May 9, 1947

After speaking on behalf of candidate Henry Wallace, Robeson sings to a group of voters from the steps of a chapel in Eugene, Oregon, on August 26, 1948.

He advocated ending the Cold War, a nonviolent fight for power between the United States and the Soviet Union, and stood for civil rights and equal justice. When he spoke in the South, he refused to speak to segregated audiences or eat in segregated restaurants. Wallace didn't think he'd really win the election, but he intended to earn enough votes to show that many Americans wanted to cooperate with the Soviet Union, and achieve world peace.

Robeson had never joined any political party. Now, at the height of his career, he campaigned for Wallace all over the country by giving concerts without pay. Robeson attracted huge numbers of black voters, and Essie campaigned for Wallace too.

In the summer of 1948, the Democrats nominated President Truman for reelection. The Republicans chose Governor Thomas Dewey of New York as their candidate. In Philadelphia, the Progressive Party nominated Henry Wallace for president. That night, Robeson spoke and sang to a crowd of 30,000 Wallace supporters and volunteers.

During the campaign, he and Brown dared to go to the Deep South—South Carolina, Georgia, and Florida. Brown, born and raised in Florida, knew the dangers they faced. As a young child, he witnessed a lynching and watched the murdered body hang for hours because no one dared move it. The experience traumatized him. "I had an intense feeling about going back there," he said. "But I didn't want to let Paul down, so I went."

When they weren't performing, Brown stayed in his room for safety and tried not to remember his early life in Florida. Robeson was uneasy too. He knew what could happen to a black man in the South. On the train ride from Jacksonville, Florida, to Savannah, Georgia, the cars were segregated into Jim Crow sections. The national treasurer of the Progressive Party, a white Southerner, who was traveling with them, stood at the entrance of the section marked "For Colored Only." Robeson snapped at him: "For God's sake stand somewhere else but here," but their companion insisted on riding with Robeson and Brown.

Black people courageously protected Robeson and Brown. When the duo was not allowed to play in public halls, they performed in black churches. Robeson's last stop in Raleigh, North Carolina, deeply moved him. This was the very place where his father had been enslaved.

On election night, November 2, 1948, as they waited for the returns, Robeson sang to hundreds of campaign workers at the Progressive Party's headquarters in New York City. By four in the morning, President Truman had a lead in the popular vote and was ahead in the Electoral College. At ten-thirty in the morning, Dewey was convinced he had lost and sent a congratulatory telegram to Truman. Robeson, perhaps overly trustful, said, "I do not fear the next four years," but he knew that President Truman opposed communists and their sympathizers.

Meanwhile, Hoover tightened his grip. When Robeson set off on a concert tour in Jamaica and Trinidad, FBI agents went with him to watch for evidence of "non-musical" activities. Hoover specifically requested that his New York office update its file on Robeson with a new report. Upon Robeson's return to the United States, FBI agents fanned out across the nation, going to every place where Robeson was scheduled to perform. They threatened that if the house managers did not cancel the concerts, they would be accused of being pro-communist subversives and put out of business. Robeson's agents had booked eighty-five engagements for him in the United States. All the performances were immediately cancelled. Record stores refused to sell Robeson's recordings, and radio stations no longer played them. Robeson was cut off from his American audience and his right to make a living as an artist. He and Brown began a four-month tour in Britain. The concerts sold out. Brown wrote to Essie, "the English public seems as fond if not fonder of Paul than ever."

In April 1949, Robeson went to Paris to speak at the World Congress of Partisans of Peace. The Congress grew from a Soviet-sponsored gathering in Poland the year before and was intended to influence world opinion in defense of peace. The two thousand delegates

Robeson addressing the World Congress of Partisans of Peace on April 20, 1949

Robeson characteristically cups his hand over his ear as he sings at the World Congress of Partisans of Peace, 1949.

from fifty countries included scientists, scholars, religious leaders, and artists.

When it was Robeson's turn at the podium, he made a spontaneous speech. "I have come among you in the name of my black brothers and of the American progressives," he began. "And I bring you a message from the Coordinating Committee of the Black Peoples of Colonial Countries." He said that America's wealth had been built "on the backs of the white workers from Europe . . . and on the backs of millions of blacks. . . . And we are resolved to share it equally. . . . Our will to fight for peace is strong. We shall not make war on anyone. We shall not make war on the Soviet Union. . . . We shall support peace and friendship among all nations." Then he sang three songs, ending with "Ol' Man River." Cheers greeted him.

But at home, Robeson's alleged words ignited a storm of criticism. The white press misquoted him as saying that black people would never fight against the Soviet Union, and labeled him a traitor. Right-wing journalists predicted that he would be "dismissed and forgotten." Some editorials demanded that he be deported to the Soviet Union. A black columnist even wrote in the *New York Amsterdam News* that Robeson was "just plain screwy." Every mainstream newspaper except the *New York Times* denounced him as an enemy of America.

Many black leaders joined whites in denouncing Robeson and denied that Robeson spoke for anyone but himself. Yet Walter White felt that "many Negroes will be glad he [Robeson] spoke as he did if it causes white Americans to wake up to the determination of Negroes to break the shackles which race prejudice fastens upon them."

No one bothered to learn whether Robeson had been quoted accurately. He had not intended to speak for all black people. In fact, some citizens liked what he had said. An editorial in a North Carolina black newspaper read, "There is hardly a Negro living in the South who, at some time or another, has not felt as Robeson expressed himself as being unwilling to lay down his life for a country that insults, lynches and restricts him to a second-class citizenship." But a *New York Times* editorial commented that Robeson was "mistaken and misled" in devoting "his life to making speeches" and suggested that he use his gifts as a concert artist instead. "We want him to sing, and to go on being Paul Robeson."

Robeson wrote to a friend: "This has been such a long, long ache that I'm numb. . . . I have read much of stuff from home. Distorted—but let it rest." From Paris, he went to the Scandinavian countries. Brown was too exhausted to make the trip, so pianist Bruno Raikin accompanied Robeson instead. The last stop was Moscow. There had been enormous changes. Robeson couldn't find Jewish friends from previous visits. Eisenstein had died and an actor-director Robeson had admired had been found brutally murdered. Disturbing newspaper accounts reported a crusade against Zionism (a movement to create a Jewish homeland in Israel). Robeson sensed an atmosphere of anti-Semitism. When he asked to see an old Jewish friend, poet Itzik Feffer, the officials escorting him were vague about Feffer's whereabouts.

Finally, on the day of the concert, the officials announced that they had found the poet, and they brought him to the hotel. As Robeson and Feffer spoke, the poet indicated with gestures that the hotel suite was bugged. Using sign language and notes written on scraps of paper, Feffer revealed that he had been imprisoned. Other old friends had been murdered. Robeson suddenly understood the reality of Stalin's purge of the Soviet Union's leading intellectuals and cultural figures whose ideas differed from the Communist Party line. He asked what he could do to help, but his friend put his finger to his lips, signaling that Robeson should keep quiet publically.

That night, Robeson's concert was broadcast to millions of Soviet people. He sang in seven languages, songs from other cultures as well as spirituals. Before singing a patriotic Soviet song, Robeson spoke about the bond between descendants of enslaved black people, like himself, and the Russian peasants (serfs) freed in 1861. The serfs had belonged to the noblemen as part of their land, but Tsar Alexander II, who hated American slavery, abolished the system of serfdom.

During the concert, Robeson humorously dedicated "Scandalize My Name" to the international press, which had maligned and misquoted him.

I met my brother the other day, gave him my right hand
And just as soon as ever my back was turned
He scandalized my name
Now do you call that a brother? No! No!
You call that a brother? No! No!
You call that a brother? No! No!
Scandalized my name

After his first concert ban, Robeson is photographed at an airport during a European tour in 1949.

The final number was "Ol' Man River," which the Russians still called "Meesseesseeppee." At the end of the song, people shouted for more. Robeson followed Russian custom and applauded the audience, then raised his hands to ask for quiet. He spoke about his meeting with his friend Feffer; he heard gasps from the audience, which included many Jewish intellectuals. For an encore, Robeson announced that he would sing the song of the Jewish partisans who had fought and died in the Warsaw Ghetto Uprising when they fearlessly resisted the Germans. He sang it first in Yiddish, then in Russian. Some people sobbed; others rushed up to touch Robeson's hand.

On this trip to Moscow, Robeson worried about the disappearance of many people dear to him. Yet, addressing a crowd at Gorky Park, on the banks of the Moscow River, he said "how deeply touched and moved" he was to be "on Soviet soil again."

"I was, I am, always will be a friend of the Soviet people."

oppressed so hard

— "Go Down, Moses"

"This is an interesting welcome," said Robeson when he landed at New York's LaGuardia Airport on June 16, 1949. Twenty uniformed policemen escorted him from the plane. Under the watchful eyes of FBI agents, the police carefully searched his bags for "documents of interest," but all they could find was a music scrapbook and packages of sheet music. Reporters needled him about his speech in Paris. He was home in America, but would he be able to speak and perform?

Robeson was sympathetic to the Soviets and never criticized them openly. However, hostility between the United States and the Soviet Union had deepened during this Cold War period. Although the two nations were allies during World War II, they now distrusted each other. Americans feared the Soviets' intention to dominate Eastern Europe and spread communism.

Robeson returned to the United States in time for his son's wedding. Paul Jr. had graduated from Cornell University with a degree in electrical engineering. At Cornell, he met and fell in love with a student, Marilyn Greenberg. Her father opposed the engagement and didn't come to the wedding, but her mother approved. Essie liked Marilyn right away, and she and Robeson were supportive of the marriage.

The ceremony took place at the apartment of a Congregational minister on the afternoon of June 19. Robeson was Paul Jr.'s best man. When they arrived at the minister's address, they were mobbed by photographers, reporters, and police. The press tried to sensationalize the marriage because it was interracial.

The street was filled with hundreds of white people, "screaming all kinds of hostile things at us," recalled Marilyn. Robeson was "outraged." He told newsmen that he "resented their presence, as the wedding was private. This would cause no particular excitement in the Soviet Union," he said.

After the ceremony, the family left in taxis. A photographer opened Robeson's cab door and leaned in to take a picture. Robeson shook his fist and shouted, "I have the greatest contempt for the press. Only something within me keeps me from smashing your cameras over your heads."

Later that afternoon, Robeson and Essie appeared at a "Welcome Home" rally at the Rockland Palace in Harlem, a venue for conventions and sporting events. Five thousand black and white people cheered him. "Hello there," boomed Robeson. "It's good to be back." He sang five songs and delivered a speech. "The road has been long; the road has been hard," he said, reminiscing about his childhood in segregated Princeton. He shared recollections of standing at the very place where his father had been enslaved, and where some of his cousins were still share-croppers and unemployed tobacco workers. "I fight for the right of the Negro people and other oppressed labor-driven Americans to have decent homes, decent jobs, and the dignity that belongs to every human being!"

Then Robeson spoke of his love for the Soviet people and of their sacrifices while fighting Hitler during World War II. "They want peace," he said, "and an abundant life." Robeson reviewed the remarks he made at the World Congress of Partisans of Peace Conference. "I said it was unthinkable that the Negro people of America or elsewhere in the world could be drawn into war with the Soviet Union. I repeat it with hundred-fold emphasis. THEY WILL NOT." Robeson urged black Americans to unite in demanding a law against lynching, to win the right to vote, and to hold jobs. "We do not want to die in vain any more on foreign battlefields," he declared. "If we must die let it be in Mississippi or Georgia! Let it be wherever we are lynched and deprived of our rights as human beings!"

The next day, the mainstream media fiercely attacked his speech. Headlines read, "Loves Soviet Best, Robeson Declares." One paper ran an editorial on the front page: "It was an accident unfortunate for America that Robeson was born here."

The House Un-American Activities Committee (HUAC) decided it wanted to hear testimonies from prominent black citizens about Robeson's views. Did they agree with Robeson that American blacks should not fight in a war against the Soviet Union? The hearings began in July 1949 in Washington, DC. The final witness was baseball player Jackie Robinson. Robinson had been signed by the Brooklyn Dodgers in 1946 and the next year was the first African American to play in the major leagues. Robeson sent him a note before he appeared at the hearings, warning Robinson that the press had badly distorted his remarks at the Paris Peace Conference. When it was Robinson's turn to speak, he said that if Robeson had actually made the comment about American blacks refusing to fight in a war against Russia, it sounded "silly." Yet, said Robinson, "He has a right to his personal views." Robeson, in turn, felt that Robinson was entitled to his own opinion. He said there was "no argument between Jackie and me."

The HUAC hearings didn't stop Robeson, or slow him down. On Saturday morning, August 27, he and Brown boarded a train to Peekskill to give a benefit concert for the Harlem chapter of the Civil Rights Congress, (CRC) an organization dedicated to raising social awareness of racial injustice and battling for the civil liberties of African Americans. The government had labeled the organization subversive. Before leaving the station, Robeson called his friends who lived near Peekskill, as he had heard rumors of trouble. The president of the Peekskill Chamber of Commerce had issued a statement labeling the concert as "un-American."

Sure enough, Robeson's friends had heard reports on the radio that various veterans groups were mobilizing to protest the concert. Robeson's friends met him and Brown at the train station and brought another friend who drove Robeson to the concert site. As they approached the picnic grounds, a truck blocked their way. A jeering crowd yelled "Dirty Commie" and "Dirty kike" and threw bricks and rocks. Police and FBI agents stood on the sidelines and did nothing. Robeson was enraged and ready to fight. By now, he was "hardened to threats." His friend jumped out of her car and yelled, "Get the hell out of here! Get him to New York."

As Robeson and Brown were driven away, the angry mob attacked the concertgoers, who were mainly black. They smashed the stage and burned Ku Klux Klan crosses on a nearby hill. A burning effigy of Robeson hung from a tree. The next day, the Westchester Committee for Law and Order met and invited Robeson to return for a concert on Labor Day weekend. He accepted on the condition that the audience would be kept safe. On the morning of Sunday, September 4, four thousand union men from groups such as the Fur and Leather Workers Union, most of them war veterans, arrived to protect Robeson and the audience at the new concert site, Hollow Brook Country Club. The men stood shoulder to shoulder up and down the hills, encircling the area like a human wall. Tension mounted as the Peekskill veterans' groups paraded and carried posters and signs reading, "Wake Up America—Peekskill Did!" By midday, protesters yelled anti-Semitic and racist taunts: "We'll kill you! You'll get in but you won't get out." "Go back to Russia."

Hundreds of private cars and chartered buses carrying about twenty thousand concertgoers streamed into the area. A police helicopter circled overhead. Four ambulances stood by. The head of Robeson's security team spotted a sniper in the hills and suggested that Robeson sing through a loudspeaker system so he'd be out of sight. Robeson refused. "I came here to sing a concert, and I'll sing it like I always do." He and Brown remained in their car until two o'clock when the concert began.

Everyone joined in the national anthem. Folksinger Pete Seeger sang a few songs, including "If I Had a Hammer," a freedom song he wrote for the civil rights movement. A pianist played a piece by Chopin. Robeson and a terrified Brown climbed out of their car. Surrounded by union men, they performed "Go Down, Moses." The hecklers blew bugles and tooted horns, but they couldn't drown out Robeson's mighty voice. He sang for almost an hour, ending with "Ol' Man River": *I must keep fightin' until I'm dyin'*. The crowd rose and gave him a standing ovation.

When they were done, Robeson and Brown were whisked away in a convoy of cars that had windows shaded with blankets to ward off flying glass. People were running over to smash the car windows with rocks. Robeson's bodyguards put him on the rear floor while two trade-union bodyguards covered him with their bodies to protect him. As they pulled out, locals hurled boulders at the cars. They clubbed concertgoers who ran to their cars, which they had been forced to park fifty yards away. Housewives walked along the road batting at passing cars with sticks. State troopers did nothing. Police were beating people too.

Pete Seeger and his family drove through the exit where a white policeman directed them to turn onto a winding road. As the car rounded the bend, a young white man threw rocks "as big as tennis balls," recalled Seeger. He was sure that the police were involved. "I don't call it a riot," he said, "I call it an attack, a planned attack."

That night, Robeson stood in front of the Hotel Theresa in Harlem and "watched in silent horror, tears streaming down his face, as dozens of shattered buses arrived filled with bleeding people—women and children as well as men." The next day, he held a press conference and explained that the concert had ended in violence because "the police who were supposed to protect us, attacked and assaulted us." Tearfully, he added, "We Negroes owe a great debt to the Jewish people, who stood there by the hundreds to defend me and all of us yesterday." He was referring to the Jewish membership of the unions, who provided most of the defense force at the concert.

Robeson received threats and hate mail long after the event. Essie, usually fearless, had an alarm system installed in the house in Enfield. At night, she kept a knife near her pillow. "If anyone I don't know enters this house, I will kill him first and find out afterwards why he came here," she told a reporter.

A national debate about the "battle of Peekskill" raged for months. Even former first lady Eleanor Roosevelt denounced the "lawlessness" at Peekskill as "disgraceful" and wrote, "I dislike everything that Paul Robeson is now saying. I still believe, however, that if he wants to give a concert, or speak his mind in public, no one should prevent him from doing so."

Robeson expressed his determination to carry on and stand by the Civil Rights Congress. He said, "I shall take my voice wherever there are those who want to hear the melody of freedom or the words that might inspire hope and courage in the face of despair and fear. . . . The song of Freedom must prevail."

Despite the tension at Peekskill, Robeson sings "Ol' Man River," as union men, mostly veterans, protectively surround him.

State trooper Tom Moore restrains booing anti-communists as they jeer Paul Robeson's fans at Peekskill on September 4, 1949.

Violence breaks out at Robeson's Peekskill concert. A state trooper is helped to his feet after being hit by a rock thrown by a demonstrator.

chapter 25

sometimes i feel discouraged, and think my work's in vain

— "Balm in Gilead"

Robeson set out on a cross-country tour arranged by the Council on African Affairs, the organization that he had cofounded and was his political base. With a smile, he told reporters that, along with singing, "I'll also be saying a few words about things." But some of the places he planned to perform banned his appearance. In Chicago, all the major civic halls shut their doors to him. Instead, he sang at the Tabernacle Baptist Church on the South Side, where most of the black population lived.

> There is a balm in Gilead
> To make the wounded whole
> There is a balm in Gilead
> To heal the sin-sick soul
> Sometimes I feel discouraged
> And think my work's in vain
> And then the holy spirit
> Revives my soul again

The Los Angeles City Council termed Robeson's coming concert "an invasion" and passed a resolution to boycott the event. Hollywood gossip columnists sparked rumors that violence would erupt if Robeson appeared. He became the target of so much hostility that even the

Communist Party suggested it might be better for him to stop speaking out and just sing for a while.

In this climate of fear and paranoia, people such as Robeson who were suspected to be communist sympathizers were hounded in a witch hunt led by Wisconsin Senator Joseph R. McCarthy. With incomplete evidence, McCarthy unscrupulously accused individuals of disloyalty. He delivered a speech claiming that communists riddled the federal government. The *New York Times* labeled the attack "indiscriminate character assassination."

Senator Joseph McCarthy sits at his desk, which is piled high with letters from supporters of his crusade against alleged security risks, 1950.

Still, anti-communist hysteria mounted. McCarthy's friend and advisor was J. Edgar Hoover. Hoover ordered his staff to give McCarthy FBI files to back up his charges, and they worked together. McCarthy's list of subversives included Americans who had formed the Abraham

Lincoln Brigade and had fought in the Spanish Civil War. These were the very men Robeson had visited and sung to during that war.

Robeson represented two things McCarthy and Hoover mistakenly encouraged Americans to fear—black people and red communist sympathizers. In March 1950, Robeson was scheduled to appear on Eleanor Roosevelt's television program discussing "the Negro in American Political Life." A barrage of criticism flooded NBC. The American Legion and the Catholic War Veterans demanded that he not be allowed to speak to protect "decent Americans" from anti-American propaganda. Within twenty-four hours, the station cancelled his appearance. Mrs. Roosevelt gave in to the decision and said that NBC had "the final say on these things."

Robeson didn't criticize Mrs. Roosevelt, but he blamed NBC. The banning of his appearance, he said, was "a sad commentary on our professions of democracy." Marie Seton said that he was "deeply hurt on many occasions," but "he never showed a trace of bitterness in public."

Despite the boycott against him, Robeson used his voice to sing and shout. On April 15, 1950, he gave a concert at Carnegie Hall. The concert celebrated the left-wing Yiddish newspaper *Morning Freiheit*, so he opened with several Yiddish songs. "Shlof, Mein Kind" ("Sleep, My Child") is a lullaby. Robeson sang it in his deepest voice, tenderly, and at the end, almost in a whisper. After the performance, fans greeted him in his dressing room. A high school student asked him for a brief statement about his life that he could use in a term paper. Robeson spoke slowly as the student took notes. "The basic mainspring of my life," he said, "is the deep struggle for the freedom of my people. . . . I have many friends all over the world, but I spring from an American heritage and I feel that my fight should be here in America for my people. I feel that all people have the right to human dignity."

In May, Robeson made a brief trip to London and attended a meeting of the World Peace Council (WPC), of which he was a member. The international organization had emerged from the World Peace Congress

With great charm, Robeson performed at a concert in Albany, New York.

and continued to promote peaceful coexistence. Robeson sang Chinese, Russian, and American songs and told the crowd that the working class in America was in danger of losing its civil liberties.

Back in the states, he addressed a thousand delegates to the National Labor Conference for Negro Rights. "What is the greatest menace in your life?" he asked in a thunderous voice. "Jim-Crow Justice! Mob Rule! Segregation! Job Discrimination!"

He criticized President Truman for portraying communism as the enemy of democracy. "Our enemies are the lynchers, the profiteers . . . the atom-bomb maniacs and the war-makers," he cried. But a few weeks later, the United States was involved in another war.

On June 25, 1950, the Korean War broke out when North Korean communist troops invaded South Korea. President Truman sent American forces to South Korea to defend Syngman Rhee's puppet government. The communists called Rhee a figurehead without any real power because his anti-communist stand won him support from the American military. At a civil rights rally at Madison Square Garden, Robeson spoke out against Truman's intervention in Korea. "The place for the Negro people to fight for their freedom is here at home," he said. FBI agents and the State Department recorded his remarks.

By this time, Robeson "was fully aware that his every act was watched and that his telephone was tapped," wrote Seton. An agent watched his home, followed him wherever he went and noted the people he spoke to. Robeson recognized the plainclothesmen and didn't try to avoid them. When friends urged him not to go out without a bodyguard, he rejected the idea of using one, except for when he was attending public meetings. Paul Jr. said, "FBI agents intruded on family and friends."

Robeson had planned to return to Europe at the end of the summer, but the State Department issued a "stop notice" at all ports, to prevent him from leaving. Hoover also ordered FBI agents to take away his passport. The agents went to the apartment of Robeson's friends, where he had recently been living, but were told he wasn't there. They waited outside all night and when Robeson didn't show up, they contacted the Council on African Affairs that Robeson had cofounded. Through the director of the Council, Robeson planned to meet the agents in his lawyer's office on July 28. The agents demanded that Robeson give them his passport, but on advice from his lawyer, Bob Rockmore, Robeson declined.

On August 4, the State Department immediately notified immigration and custom officials that Robeson's passport was cancelled. The reason they gave was vague. "The Department considers that Paul Robeson's travel abroad at this time would be contrary to the best interests of the United States." The world's beloved singer and champion of peace was being shut down, virtually a prisoner in his own country.

When Robeson and his lawyer asked why it would be "detrimental" for him to travel, they were told that his frequent criticism of the treatment of black people in America should not be discussed in foreign countries. It was a "family affair." Robeson's lawyers said this was an unconstitutional violation of the right of free speech. The State Department said they could take up the matter in court.

Two weeks later, Robeson and his team of lawyers met with passport officials in Washington. The officials said they would consider returning his passport if he signed a statement saying that he would not make any speeches overseas. Robeson refused to give up his right to speak and said this was one more attempt by the Truman administration "to silence the protests of the Negro people." He pointed out that he needed his passport in order to give concerts and earn a living.

In December 1950, his lawyer filed a lawsuit against the State Department to regain his passport. The biggest fight of Robeson's life had just begun.

chapter 26 nobody knows my sorrow

— "Nobody Knows the Trouble I've Seen"

As Robeson was walking down the street in Harlem, a well-wisher stopped to say hello and asked, "Paul, were you born in Russia?" Robeson laughed. The question reflected public belief that anyone "who fights for peace . . . for friendship with the Soviet Union, for labor's rights and for full equality for Negroes now, cannot be a 'real' American." Robeson decided to share his feelings about world affairs in "Here's My Story," a column in the monthly journal *Freedom* that he helped start. He began by writing about his father's "slave origin," and the family's poverty when his father lost his ministry.

In recounting his struggles and achievements, Robeson wrote, "I refuse to let my personal success, as part of a fraction of one per cent of the Negro people, to explain away the injustices to fourteen million of my people; because with all the energy at my command, I fight for the right of the Negro people and other oppressed labor-driven Americans to have decent homes, decent jobs, and the dignity that belongs to every human being!" His words sparked greater hostility and intensified Hoover's harassment. Would he ever regain his passport and be free to travel and earn a living as an international performer?

Shunned by all concert agencies, Robeson remained undaunted, and instead appeared at cultural events, civil rights meetings, and peace rallies. In Chicago, in 1951, he sang at a huge peace conference and spoke about civil liberties. Robeson warned that jailing communist opponents

210

of American policies posed a threat to the First Amendment of the Constitution, which protected freedom of speech. After the conference, Charlie Parker, the jazz musician, approached him and said, "I just wanted to shake your hand. You're a great man."

In January 1952, Robeson was scheduled to give a concert in Vancouver, British Columbia. He had been invited by the International Union of Mine, Mill, and Smelter Workers of British Columbia. A three-car caravan drove Robeson from Seattle, Washington, to Blaine, at the border. Americans didn't need passports to cross in and out of Canada. But the State Department knew about the concert and arranged to prevent Robeson from leaving the United States. Immigration officials stopped him at the border and he returned to Seattle.

The miners were indignant and hatched a plan with Robeson. They hooked up a long-distance telephone connection relayed to the public-address system. The next day, Robeson sat a desk in a Seattle union office and performed. The two thousand miners in Vancouver heard him sing "Joe Hill." Robeson gave a speech saying that the American government was keeping him in "a sort of domestic house arrest." The miners responded by asking him to come back in May and give an "across-the-border" concert at the Peace Arch, a monument on the border between Canada and the United States. Robeson accepted.

On May 18, 1952, on the United States' side of the border, Robeson climbed onto the rear of a flatbed truck, where Larry Brown sat at an upright piano. Five thousand people gathered on the American side of the park, and thirty thousand Canadians assembled on the other side. FBI agents were there too, and filmed and photographed the event while the Border Patrol took down license plate numbers of the Americans' cars. Photographers also took pictures of Robeson grinning and waving his hand at the international boundary marker. He was determined to be heard.

Ignoring the FBI, Robeson spoke into the public-address system, which carried his voice across the border. "I can't tell you how moved

I am at this moment," he said. "It seems nothing can keep me from my beloved friends in Canada. You have known me through many years. I am the same Paul, fighting a little harder because the times call for harder struggles." He opened the program by singing "Every Time I Feel the Spirit," with Brown joining in. Then, "Joe Hill." Robeson introduced "No More Auction Block for Me" by saying that it "comes from the very depths of the struggle of my people in America." He told how the spiritual was often heard at the A.M.E. Zion Church where his father and then his brother served as ministers.

> *No more driver's lash for me*
> *No more, no more*
> *No more driver's lash for me*
> *Many thousands gone.*

The sponsors of the Peace Arch Concert invited him back the following year, but all of his other concert dates were cancelled except at black churches throughout the country. At the Hartford Avenue Baptist Church in Detroit, in 1952, he told the congregation, "What would my father say to me if he were alive? He would say, 'It's hard, son. But don't forget I was born in slavery. And your people were not able to do anything as free people for a long time. . . . So you stand your ground. . . . Just keep your courage and keep your heart.'"

Robeson did just that. Although his income had dropped drastically, he still earned money from the sales of his recordings overseas. His legal battles to win back his passport were expensive. Essie was forced to sell the house in Enfield. For a while, she stayed with her son and daughter-in-law, and then she moved into a residential hotel. Although she and Robeson were still married, they had lived separately for a long time. Essie continued to travel, lecture, and publish articles as a scholar and activist. Robeson stayed with various friends, then spent a year with his brother Ben at the A.M.E. Zion Church parsonage in Harlem. Ben

Robeson performs at a Christmas party at Rev. Mother Lena M. Stokes's Church in Harlem. The photographer's son, Ken Davidoff, leans closer to listen. Ken's grandmother did charity work for the church.

converted one of his studies into a bedroom for his brother, and installed a seven-foot bed and a spinet piano. "Paul felt safe there," wrote Paul Jr.

In December, the Soviet Union announced that it was awarding Robeson its International Stalin Prize for Strengthening Peace Among Peoples, established in honor of Stalin's seventieth birthday, and presented to citizens of any country for outstanding service in "the struggle against war." The award came with a gold medal and $25,000 ($227,766 in 2018 dollars). The State Department still retained Robeson's passport and wouldn't permit him to receive the award. Instead, the award was presented to him the following year at Harlem's Hotel Theresa before three hundred guests. Robeson accepted the award "in the name of the American fighters for peace."

Essie's ties with the Soviet Union also brought her under scrutiny.

Because of her pro-Soviet statements in her book, *African Journey*, Senator McCarthy's Senate investigating committee summoned her to appear on July 7, 1953. The committee counsel, Roy M. Cohn, began the questioning by asking, "You are Mrs. Paul Robeson, is that correct?" Essie replied, "Yes, and very proud of it too."

When asked if she was a member of the Communist Party, she refused to answer, citing the Fifth and Fifteenth Amendments to the Constitution. Senator McCarthy said that the Fifteenth Amendment dealt only with her right to vote as an American citizen. Essie replied, "I don't quite understand your statement that we are all American citizens . . . I am a second-class citizen now, as a Negro." She stated that many southern black people were denied the right to vote because of unjust laws and customs enforced by white people.

A member of the committee said that Essie's refusal to answer meant that there was "a good chance" that she was a communist, because she believed that "race has not had a fair deal in the United States." Essie said, "The reason I refuse to answer the question is because . . . my opinions are my private personal affair." Responding to a question about her husband's political activities, she shot back, "Why don't you ask him?"

Paul Jr. was suspected too. Because of his name, he could not find work as an engineer, so he used his Russian language skills to translate scientific journals. In late 1953, Paul Jr., Robeson, and his friend Lloyd Brown formed a record company, Othello Recording Corporation. Paul Jr. served as president and producer. They recorded three albums, including one that featured Robeson singing church hymns. No commercial distributors would market the albums, and no radio stations would play them, so they sold the records using mail order and through black churches.

Paul Jr. set up an informal system so that they could record Robeson's songs in various venues, like friends' living rooms, on short notice.

Expert engineers gave their services. Since Lawrence Brown felt he could no longer cope with the problems involved in performing with Robeson, he made only selective appearances. Alan Booth, a talented pianist, also performed with him. Paul Jr. picked out the final takes with his father. Sometimes, Robeson altered the lyrics to emphasize his views. In "Jacob's Ladder," "soldiers of the cross" became "soldiers of the fight." These recording sessions temporarily lifted Robeson's spirits and distracted him from his passport battle.

Offers for him to give concerts kept coming in from England, Russia, Canada, Israel, and Mexico. A theater in London wanted him to do a run of *Othello*. Without a passport, though, he couldn't travel. In Harlem, a group of fellow artists held a "Salute to Paul Robeson" and supported his right to regain his passport. In England, a Paul Robeson Committee was formed and launched a "Let Robeson Sing" campaign. Students at City College of New York, and Swarthmore College in Pennsylvania, invited him to sing and speak. High school students in New York City gathered to hear him talk about his fight, and they signed a petition demanding that his passport be returned. Robeson expressed delight at the overflow crowds. He saw "the stirrings of new life" among these young people.

Nonetheless, the State Department rejected his application to regain his passport. Robeson was not the only one striving to make changes at this time. Lawyer Thurgood Marshall was fighting in the courts to challenge the "separate but equal" doctrine to end school segregation in the United States. In 1952, Marshall and his team argued their case before the Supreme Court and presented their arguments again in 1953. At last in 1954 they won. The landmark decision in *Brown v. Board of Education* banned segregation in public schools.

Robeson heard the great news and felt inspired. To him, the ruling was a "magnificent stride forward," yet he warned black people everywhere to "fight to see that it is enforced." Sure enough, many Southern states refused to accept the Supreme Court's decision and did not desegregate

At a left-wing meeting in Union Square, New York, on May 2, 1954, Robeson sings before addressing the audience.

From left to right: Attorney George E. C. Hayes, Thurgood Marshall, and James Nabrit on the steps of the Supreme Court Building, congratulating each other on the *Brown v. Board of Education* decision. May 17, 1954.

their schools. A year later, Marshall and his lawyers had to return to the Supreme Court and outline a plan for implementing the Court's ruling. The civil rights campaign was spreading throughout the South and gathering strength.

In Montgomery, Alabama, Rosa Parks refused to give up her seat to a white person and move to the back of a bus. She was arrested, and thousands gathered to protest. Reverend Dr. Martin Luther King Jr., the new minister at Dexter Avenue Baptist Church, spoke and became president of the Montgomery Improvement Association to launch and oversee a bus boycott.

Robeson cheered silently from the sidelines. He didn't want to jeopardize the burgeoning civil rights movement due to the government's labeling of him as a subversive. He also had few outlets for singing or speaking to express support. He considered himself a "forerunner" of the movement rather than a "participant."

His own long battle continued into the summer of 1955. Robeson had grown optimistic when the State Department said he could travel to Canada. However, when he went to Washington, DC, in August for a hearing in the US District Court, the government's attorney argued that Robeson was "one of the most dangerous men in the world" and a threat to the security of the United States. Robeson refused to sign an affidavit stating that he was not a communist, saying that it was unconstitutional. He would not sign a document other Americans were not asked to sign.

Robeson remained "a prisoner in his native land." The unrelenting hatred and hostility directed at him wore him down physically and emotionally. In October 1955, he underwent surgery for a prostate condition and stayed in the hospital for three weeks. Essie also suffered serious health problems and needed a mastectomy to combat breast cancer. When they both began recovering, they decided to buy a Harlem brownstone at 16 Jumel Terrace and live together again.

By May 1956, Robeson showed more signs of strain. Usually upbeat and vigorous, he became weak and deeply depressed. He stayed in his suite of rooms in the brownstone, seeing no one but his family, and refused to consult a psychiatrist. "Suddenly everything changed," wrote Paul Jr.

On May 22, word came from Washington that Robeson had been subpoenaed to testify at a hearing of the House Un-American Activities Committee. His doctors advised him not to go, begging him to stay home. They wanted to request a postponement for medical reasons. The House Committee granted a delay until June 12. The doctors still felt that Robeson was not well enough to appear and wanted to request a postponement. Robeson insisted on making the trip. He had been threatened all his life and had never backed down. He wouldn't start now.

we're soldiers in this fight

chapter 27

— "Jacob's Ladder"

On June 12, 1956, Robeson sat in the hearing room of the House Office Building waiting to be called as a witness. His two lawyers and Essie and Paul Jr. were with him. At first, "he slumped in his chair, looking desolate," recalled Paul Jr. Essie worried that Robeson couldn't handle the questioning. She decided to pretend to faint if his testimony seemed to be "going haywire." But as soon as Robeson's name was called, "he sat bolt upright . . . and strode rapidly to his witness seat" and was "defiant from the outset."

Robeson testifying before the HUAC (House Un-American Activities Committee) in Washington, DC, June 12, 1956

219

"Are you now a member of the Communist Party?" asked Richard Arens, the committee's staff director. "Oh, please," said Robeson. Arens told him to answer the question. "What do you mean by [the Communist Party]?" said Robeson. "As far as I know it is a legal party." Arens repeated the question. Robeson said, "Would you like to come to the ballot box when I vote and take out the ballot and see?"

Then Arens accused Robeson of being a member of the Communist Party under an assumed name—"John Thomas." Robeson burst out laughing. "My name is Paul Robeson, and anything I have to say, or stand for, I have said in public all over the world." Arens said, "I put it to you as a fact, and ask you to affirm or deny the fact, that your Communist Party name was 'John Thomas.'" Robeson said, "I invoke the Fifth Amendment. This is really ridiculous." Robeson had brought a prepared statement and wanted to read it. Arens asked him what communists had helped him prepare it. Again, Robeson invoked the Fifth Amendment, then said, "I am not being tried for whether I am a communist. I am being tried for fighting for the rights of my people, who are still second-class citizens in this United States of America."

Questioning went on for an hour. The sharpest exchange came when Robeson praised the Soviet Union. He said, "In Russia I felt for the first time like a full human being. No color prejudice like in Mississippi, no color prejudice like in Washington. . . . I did not feel the pressure of color as I feel [it] in this committee today."

"Why do you not stay in Russia?" asked Representative Gordon H. Scherer.

"Because my father was a slave," said Robeson, "and my people died to build this country, and I am going to stay here and have a part of [it] just like you. And no fascist-minded people will drive me from it. Is that clear?" Scherer asked why Robeson had sent his son to school in Russia. And Robeson said "to spare him from racial prejudice."

"What prejudice are you talking about?" asked another member of the committee. "You were graduated from Rutgers." Robeson explained that "the success of a few Negroes" like Jackie Robinson and himself did not make up for the thousands of black families in the South still living in poverty and a kind of semi-slavery.

As insults flew back and forth, Robeson quietly controlled his anger. In a lowered, firm voice he told the committee members that *they* were the true "un-Americans" and should be ashamed of themselves. Chairman Francis Walter furiously banged down his gavel and adjourned the hearing. "You should adjourn this forever," said Robeson, having the last word.

Outside the building, reporters hounded him. "I answered every question," he said. "I was just standing my ground." Unbeknownst to Robeson, the committee voted unanimously to recommend that he be cited for contempt of Congress.

The hearing had rejuvenated him. Back in New York, he received congratulations and messages from political fans and supporters. "Mr. Robeson is Right," read a headline in the *Afro-American*. The editorial agreed that the House members could better spend their time passing civil rights measures and questioning white supremacists.

Invigorated, Robeson returned to work. He asked Lloyd Brown, a leftist black journalist, to assist him in writing *Here I Stand*, a book about his childhood and beliefs. "I hope to very soon resume my career as an actor and singer," he said. "I still have a pretty good voice rolling around."

By 1958, things were indeed better for Robeson. He embarked on his first concert tour on professional stages across the country and recorded a new commercial album for Vanguard Records. He told a reporter, "I am sorry now that I quit the concert stage because of politics. . . . Any 'politics' in the future will be in my singing."

The FBI supported the fantasy that Robeson's efforts to present an acceptable image to the mainstream black community was for the purpose of taking over the leadership of the NAACP. But the truth was that Robeson had never had any influence in the NAACP. The leadership of the organization had purposely distanced themselves from Robeson to protect the NAACP and their civil rights work.

After a concert in San Francisco, music critics wrote, "the years have done virtually nothing to the greatest natural basso voice of the present generation." He recorded the new album for Vanguard, the first time in seven years that he'd been in a commercial studio. Although Robeson was "nervous as a cat," wrote Essie, he "was never in better voice."

On April 9, 1958, he celebrated his sixtieth birthday and received greetings and tributes from all over the world. His friend Nehru, now Prime Minister of an independent India, issued plans for a government-sponsored celebration. Nehru hailed Robeson not only because he was a great artist, but also "because he has represented and suffered for a cause which should be dear to all of us—the cause of human dignity."

Robeson's cross-country tour ended in New York on May 9, 1958, at Carnegie Hall. The concert was sold out. Fifteen policemen were stationed at the hall, but there were no disturbances. As soon as Robeson strode onstage, the crowd cheered. This time, Alan Booth accompanied him. Varying the tempo, he sang the English tune "Oh, No, John," and then the "Hassidic Chant" [Kaddish] in Hebrew and in English. The program included his traditional favorites—"Water Boy," "Balm in Gilead," and "Every Time I Feel the Spirit."

Robeson mixed songs with comments, reminiscences, and even a bit of dancing. The concert also featured the closing speech of *Othello*. Robeson ended with "Jacob's Ladder," and said to the audience, "Join me." Together, they sang:

> *We are climbing Jacob's ladder*
> *We are climbing Jacob's ladder*
> *We are climbing Jacob's ladder*
> *Soldiers of the cross.*

The audience rose to their feet shouting and whistling, demanding encores and curtain calls. Robeson was gratified by his reception and thrilled to be performing again. Although critics noted that his voice had "lost much of its old glow," they praised his "incomparable vigor of presentation and limitless charm."

Since most of the audience had been white, Robeson scheduled a second concert at Carnegie Hall on May 23. He arranged to have hundreds of tickets distributed throughout Harlem. The concert sold out immediately.

Two weeks later, Robeson gave a daytime concert at his brother Ben's church. Larry Brown accompanied him. Robeson told the overflow crowd, "I want the folks of Mother Zion to know that a lot of the hard struggle is over and that my concert career has practically been reestablished. . . . I've been waiting for this afternoon just to come back to give my thanks here."

Robeson raises his voice in song from the pulpit of the A.M.E. Mother Zion Church in Harlem, pastored by his brother Ben.

On June 16, 1958, he received the news he had been hoping for. The Supreme Court announced that in the case of the artist Rockwell Kent, which also applied to Robeson (they had both been denied passports because of their political views), the U.S. Secretary of State had no right to deny a passport to citizens on the basis of their political beliefs. The Passport Division had no right to demand that an applicant sign an affidavit concerning membership in the Communist Party.

Nine days later, the State Department issued Robeson's passport. Smiling, he held it up so that photographers could get good pictures. "A wonderful thing has happened," he said. "I have won the struggle in my own country to regain my rights." Robeson said his victory was not just a personal one, but "a victory for the 'other America.'" He thanked his lawyer, "and, of course, the Supreme Court for what has happened, and also the thousands and thousands of people of all races and creeds who have been my well–wishers all these years in the struggle for a passport."

For five years, he delighted audiences in the British Isles, the Soviet Union, Australia, and New Zealand. But with this hectic schedule, he suffered from exhaustion and episodes of depression. Mental and physical problems finally forced him to stop performing. After a suicide attempt in Moscow, he was rushed to the hospital, and later treated in a psychiatric nursing home in London, and at a clinic in East Berlin. Essie wrote to a friend, "The long years of doing too much in too many places has taken its toll." When his brother Ben died on August 22, 1964, he was too sick to go to the funeral.

Essie and Robeson returned to New York on December 22, 1963. He wanted to see his family. When reporters asked if he would take part in the civil rights struggle, he said, "I've been a part of the civil rights movement all my life."

In August 1964, at the height of Freedom Summer, and a campaign in Mississippi to help black people register to vote, he issued a statement

Robeson happily examines his new passport, June 1958.

Cupping his hand over his ear and holding a bouquet of flowers he has just received upon arrival at the London Airport (now Heathrow) in the summer of 1958, Robeson sings for his fans. Essie, on the left, smiles at the warm welcome.

Family portrait, 1957: Robeson holds his grandchildren Susan and David on his lap; standing behind them are Marilyn Robeson, Essie, and Paul Jr.

to the press. "While I must continue my temporary retirement from public life, I am of course deeply involved with the great upsurge of our people. Like all of you, my heart has been filled with admiration for the many thousands of Negro Freedom Fighters and their white associates who are waging the battle for civil rights throughout the country and especially in the South."

At an event celebrating Robeson's sixty-seventh birthday, John Lewis, the young black chairman of S.N.C.C. (Student Non-Violent Coordinating Committee), gave the keynote address. He said, "We of S.N.C.C. are Paul Robeson's spiritual children."

Robeson was pleased when Congress, under the leadership of

President Lyndon B. Johnson, passed the Civil Rights Act of 1964, and the Voting Rights Act of 1965. But he slid into a downward cycle emotionally and expressed suicidal thoughts in a moment at Jumel Terrace. His psychiatrist said that with all the hostility Robeson had endured, it was surprising he had not broken down sooner. The doctor also said that organic changes in his brain were causing symptoms of mental disease.

In August, Essie needed treatment for cancer. While she was gone, Robeson suffered another bout of depression. By September, they were both home at Jumel Terrace. One night, Robeson walked out and disappeared. The next morning, he was found near Highbridge Park, a few blocks from home, confused. He was later hospitalized.

After his release, Paul Jr. took him to his sister's house in Philadelphia. He felt comfortable there, and Marian took wonderful care of him. One of her friends dropped by a few times a week to accompany him on the piano. Robeson sang his favorites. But he was thinner, frailer, and not his old self. Often he would sit in silence. While he was in Philadelphia, Essie returned to the hospital. Her cancer had spread throughout her body. She died on December 13, 1965. Robeson was unable to attend the funeral. For the next ten years, he continued living with Marian and saw a few visitors.

On December 28, 1975, Robeson suffered a slight stroke, and then a series of strokes. On January 23, 1976, Paul Robeson died at the age of seventy-seven. The *New York Times* featured an obituary summarizing Robeson's career on the front page. The *Amsterdam News* ran a big headline reading, "Goodbye, Paul!"

Mourners viewed Robeson's body at Benta's Funeral Home in Harlem. His recordings of "Amazing Grace" and "Ol' Man River" played softly in the chapel. More than five thousand people attended his funeral at A.M.E. Zion Church. An overflow crowd of thousands stood outside in the rain. Lloyd Brown eulogized Robeson and said, "The tallest tree in our forest has fallen." "Deep River" played as the pallbearers carried out the coffin.

Robeson's ashes were buried beside Essie's grave at the Ferncliff Cemetery in Hartsdale, New York. His gravesite is marked by a simple bronze plaque engraved with words he once spoke: "The artist must elect to fight for freedom or slavery. I have made my choice. I had no alternative."

For some years, Robeson was forgotten. Eventually, the world began remembering the extraordinary singer, actor, scholar, athlete, and political activist. His son Paul Jr. collected his writings, recordings, scrapbooks, letters, and photos in an archive, and published a biography of his father. Robeson's records were reissued as CDs. Some of his movies were transferred to DVDs. YouTube shows clips of him singing and acting.

In Princeton, the house where he was born is being restored as a museum and community center. Next door, on Witherspoon Street, stands the Paul Robeson Center for the Arts. A street nearby was renamed Paul Robeson Place. His sister Marian's house, where he spent his last years, is a museum and National Historic Landmark. New York designated his former apartment building at 555 Edgecombe Avenue in Harlem to be a National Historic Landmark, and renamed the building The Paul Robeson Residence. Edgecombe Avenue has been co-named Paul Robeson Avenue.

Rutgers University honored his memory with the Paul Robeson Campus Center to create a sense of belonging for students of color, and offer them social, cultural, and career development activities. The Paul Robeson Campus Center at Rutgers University–Newark serves the predominantly commuter student body, and provides a venue for community gatherings. Another monument on the New Brunswick campus is the Paul Robeson Plaza, a reunion gift from the class of 1971 that was dedicated on April 12, 2019. The plaza is located on the very ground where Robeson attended classes, and features black granite panels etched with his words, and pictures of him, to inspire future generations. Rutgers established the Paul Robeson Leadership

Institute to help students who are the first in their family to attend college prepare for the experience and succeed.

In one of his last interviews, Robeson said, "There is more, much more, that needs to be done, of course, before we can reach our goals." He left a legacy of commitment to civil rights, global freedom, and music as a universal language to bring people together. With courage, he fought for his beliefs and never backed down. Not only did he sing spirituals, he lived them.

Didn't my Lord deliver Daniel?
And why not every man?
The moon runs down in a purple stream
The sun refuse to shine
Every star did disappear
Yes, freedom shall be mine

acknowledgments

At a writers' workshop, I casually mentioned that I had once met Paul Robeson, and the workshop leader, Carolyn Yoder, immediately said that she had always wanted to do a biography of Robeson. She grew up in Princeton, New Jersey, Robeson's hometown. It was serendipity. I thank my editor Carolyn, and the team at Calkins Creek/Boyds Mills Press, for helping me produce this book.

Special thanks to the Robeson Family Trust. I am grateful to my agent, Kevin O'Connor, for advising me in research and writing. Many thanks go to independent scholar Shirleen Robinson for her careful review of the manuscript and her insightful comments.

I am indebted to the librarians and staff at the Schomburg Center for Research in Black Culture, particularly Andrea Battleground, Linden Anderson Jr., Michael Mery, and Christopher Stahling, who guided me on a walking tour of Robeson sites in Harlem. From the Billy Rose Theatre Division of the New York Public Library, I am grateful to Tom Lisanti, Jeremy Megraw, and David Callahan.

I thank Joellen ElBashir and Meaghan Alston from the Moorland-Spingarn Research Center. A big thank you goes to Stephanie Schwartz at the Historical Society of Princeton. At Rutgers University Libraries, I owe appreciation to Erica Gorder in Special Collections and University Archives; Albert C. King, Curator of Manuscripts and Special Collections; and Tom Frusciano. Many people generously helped me obtain photo permissions. I am grateful to Clive Debenham and Dr. Margaret Debenham, heirs of photographer J. W. Debenham; Dr. Edward Burns, Successor Trustee of the Carl Van Vechten Trust; and Sara Davidoff, widow of photographer Bob Davidoff.

I greatly enjoyed interviewing Shirley Satterfield, a historian and educator in Princeton, who met Robeson when she was a little girl and grew up in his neighborhood. I also appreciated talking to Vernoca L. Michael, Executive Coordinator of The Paul Robeson House in Philadelphia, the home of his sister Marian, where he spent his last years.

Acknowledgments would be incomplete without heartfelt thanks to my writer friends at "Lunch Bunch," who critiqued draft after draft, and my writer friends at Third Act for their boundless encouragement and support. Of course, a huge thank you goes to my husband Michael, for lovingly standing by, and to our son Andrew, who patiently helped me download images and solve computer problems on an almost daily basis.

Most of all, I thank Paul Robeson for his voice, his courage, and his inspiration.

bibliography*

All websites active at time of publication

books

Bogle, Donald. *Bright Boulevards, Bold Dreams: The Story of Black Hollywood.* New York: Ballantine Books, 2006.

Boyle, Sheila Tully, and Andrew Bunie. *Paul Robeson: The Years of Promise and Achievement.* Amherst: University of Massachusetts Press, 2001.

Brown, Lloyd L. *The Young Paul Robeson: On My Journey Now.* Boulder, CO: Westview Press, 1997.

Cunningham, Kevin. *J. Edgar Hoover: Controversial FBI Director.* Minneapolis, MN: Compass Point Books, 2006.

Decker, Todd. *Show Boat: Performing Race in an American Musical.* New York: Oxford University Press, 2013.

Duberman, Martin. *Paul Robeson: A Biography.* New York: The New Press, 1989.

Dyja, Thomas. *Walter White: The Dilemma of Black Identity in America.* The Library of African-American Biography series. Chicago: Ivan R. Dee, 2008.

Fordin, Hugh. *Getting to Know Him: A Biography of Oscar Hammerstein II.* New York: Da Capo Press, 1995.

Gentry, Curt. *J. Edgar Hoover: The Man and the Secrets.* New York: W.W. Norton & Company, 1991.

Giblin, James Cross. *The Life and Death of Adolf Hitler.* New York: Clarion Books, 2002.

Giblin, James Cross. *The Rise and Fall of Senator Joe McCarthy.* New York: Clarion Books, 2009.

Goodman, Jordan. *Paul Robeson: A Watched Man.* New York: Verso, 2013.

Gordon, Linda. *The Second Coming of the KKK: The Ku Klux Klan of the 1920s and the American Political Tradition.* New York: Liveright Publishing Corporation, a Division of W.W. Norton & Company, 2017.

Greenfield, Eloise. *Paul Robeson.* Illustrated by George Ford. New York: Lee & Low Books, 2009.

Hill, Errol G., and James V. Hatch. *A History of African American Theatre (Cambridge Studies in American Theatre and Drama)*. New York: Cambridge University Press, 2013.

Hughes, Langston. *The Big Sea, An Autobiography*. American Century series. New York: Hill and Wang, 1993.

Isaacs, Edith J.R. *The Negro in the American Theatre*. New York: Theatre Arts, 1947.

Johnson, James Weldon. *Black Manhattan*. New York: Da Capo Press, 1991.

Kendi, Ibram X. *Stamped from the Beginning: The Definitive History of Racist Ideas in America*. New York: Nation Books, 2016.

Lane, Stewart F. *Black Broadway: African Americans on the Great White Way*. Garden City Park, NY: Square One Publishers, 2015.

Lubasch, Arnold H. *Robeson: An American Ballad*. Lanham, MD: Rowman & Littlefield, 2012.

Neruda, Pablo. *Let the Rail Splitter Awake and Other Poems*. New York: International Publishers, 1970, 1988.

Payne, Charles M. *I've Got the Light of Freedom: The Organizing Tradition and the Mississippi Freedom Struggle*. Berkeley: University of California Press, 2007.

Peters, Margot. *Mrs. Pat: The Life of Mrs. Patrick Campbell*. London: Bodley Head, 1984.

Rampersad, Arnold. *The Life of Langston Hughes: Volume I: 1902–1941*. New York: Oxford University Press, 1986.

Rampersad Arnold, and David Roessel, eds. *The Collected Poems of Langston Hughes*. Vintage Classics series. New York: Vintage Books, 1995.

Ransby, Barbara. *Eslanda: The Large and Unconventional Life of Mrs. Paul Robeson*. New Haven: Yale University Press, 2013.

Robeson, Eslanda Goode. *Paul Robeson, Negro*. New York: Harper & Brothers, 1930.

Robeson, Paul, with Lloyd L. Brown. *Here I Stand*. Boston: Beacon Press, 1988.

Robeson, Paul. *Paul Robeson Speaks: Writings, Speeches, Interviews, 1918–1974*. Philip S. Foner, ed. New York: Brunner/Mazel, Inc., a Citadel Press Book, 1978.

Robeson, Paul Jr. *The Undiscovered Paul Robeson: An Artist's Journey, 1898-1939*. New York: Wiley, 2001.

Robeson, Paul Jr. *The Undiscovered Paul Robeson: Quest for Freedom, 1939–1976.* Hoboken, NJ: Wiley, 2010.

Robeson, Susan. *Grandpa Stops a War: A Paul Robeson Story.* Illustrated by Rod Brown. New York: Triangle Square, 2019.

Robeson, Susan. *The Whole World in His Hands: A Pictorial Biography of Paul Robeson.* Secaucus, NJ: Citadel Press, 1981.

Rubin, Susan Goldman. *Brown v. Board of Education: A Fight for Simple Justice.* New York: Holiday House, 2016.

Sarna, Jonathan D. *American Judaism. A History.* New Haven: Yale University Press, 2004.

Seton, Marie. *Paul Robeson.* London: Dobson Books, 1958.

Shakespeare, William. *The Tragedie of Othello, The Moor of Venice.* New York: Applause, 2001.

Sparrow, Jeff. *No Way But This: In Search of Paul Robeson.* Melbourne, Australia: Scribe, 2017.

Stewart, Jacqueline Najuma. *Migrating to the Movies: Cinema and Black Urban Modernity.* Berkeley: University of California Press, 2005.

Stewart, Jeffrey C. *Paul Robeson: Artist and Citizen.* New Brunswick, NJ: Rutgers University Press, 1998.

Swindall, Lindsey R. *Paul Robeson: A Life of Activism and Art.* Lanham, MD: Rowman & Littlefield, 2013.

Watterson, Kathryn. *I Hear My People Singing: Voices of African American Princeton.* Princeton, NJ: Princeton University Press, 2017.

Wilkerson, Isabel. *The Warmth of Other Suns: The Epic Story of America's Great Migration.* New York: Vintage Books, A Division of Random House, Inc., 2010.

documents

Federal Bureau of Investigation File FBIHQ 100-12304, Section:1; Paul Robeson, Sr.

Rutgers College Catalog. New Brunswick, NJ: Rutgers College, 1915–1916, 1916–1917, 1917–1918, 1918–1919.

articles

Anderson, David. "Robeson and Lamont Passports Received After Seven-Year Fight." *New York Times*, June 7, 1958.

Anderson, George. "48 Hurt in Clashes at Robeson Rally; Buses Are Stoned." *New York Times*, September 5, 1949.

Broggiotti, Mary. "All American in All Languages." *New York Post*, 1950.

Broun, Heywood. "It Seems to Me." *World*, April 18, 1925.

Carter, Richard. "Robeson Home, Met by Cops, Tells Love for U.S." *Daily Compass*, June 17, 1949.

Chapman, John. "Majesty and Dignity Illuminate Negro Paul Robeson's 'Othello.'" 1942.

Coleman, Robert. "'Othello' at Shubert Is Just Terrific." *The Theatre*, 1942.

Cotter, Holland. "Remembering Lynching's Toll." *New York Times*, June 3, 2018.

Davis, George. "A Healing Hand in Harlem." *New York Times*, April 22, 1979.

Duberman, Martin. "A Giant Denied His Rightful Stature in Film." *New York Times*, March 29, 1998.

Gordon, A. J. "U.S. Cancels Robeson's Passport After He Refuses to Surrender It." *New York Times*, August 4, 1950, p. 1.

Lubasch, Arnold H. "In Harlem With: Paul Robeson Jr.; Finding His Own Voice And Learning to Use It." *New York Times*, Archives, October 21, 1993.

McClure, Brian. "Essential Brotherhood: Langston and Thurgood." Langston Hughes, Omega Psi Phi, April 17, 2011. Stateofhbcus.files.wordpress. com/2011/04/langstonhughesdesignii.jpeg.

McNulty, Charles. "A Jazz Age Baby Is Reborn." *Los Angeles Times*, Monday, April 25, 2016.

Moscow, Warren. "Robeson Backers Prepared to Fight." *New York Times*, Monday, September 5, 1949.

"Paul Robeson's Voice Rings Over Spain's Battlefield," *New York Post*. Madrid, January 28, 1939.

Poitier, Sidney. Interview, complete in MFLA 73–456, *Cineaste* V. 8 #3, Winter 1977/78.

Popper, Ellen. "A View from the Audience." *Playbill*, April 1978.

"Proud Valley—Songs of People." *Morning Telegraph*, May 19, 1941.

Robeson, Paul. "A Wonderful Thing Has Happened." *Newark News*, London, July 11, 1958.

Robeson, Paul Jr. "Reflections on My Father's Centennial." *New York Amsterdam News*, May 14–20, 1998.

Robeson, Paul Jr. "The Counterfeit 'Paul Robeson.' A Legacy Demeaned." *New York Amsterdam News*, February 3–9, 2000.

Robinson, Jackie. Text of statement. *New York Times*, July 10, 1949; August 2, 1949.

Roosevelt, Eleanor. "Mrs. Roosevelt calls outbreak 'horrible.'" *New York Herald Tribune*, September 1, 1949.

Simon, Henry W. "Robeson Returns to Carnegie Hall." *New York World Telegram*, October 7, 1940.

Smith, A. Constant. "Paul Robeson Stirs Soviet Audience." *Moscow Daily News*, December 20, 1936.

Sullivan, John Jeremiah. "American Shuffle." *New York Times Magazine*, March 27, 2016.

Tapley, Mel. "Every Artist Must Know Where He Stands." *New York Amsterdam News*, January 31, 1976.

Tuhus, Melinda. "Celebrating a Marvel Named Robeson." *New York Times*, April 5, 1998.

Van Gelder, Robert. "Robeson Remembers: An Interview with the Star of 'Othello,' Partly About His Past," c. 1949.

Wechsler, James A. "Of Triumph and Tragedy." *New York Post*, February 3, 1976.

interviews by phone, with susan goldman rubin

Michael, Vernoca L., Director, Paul Robeson House & Museum, September 14, 2017, and February 3, 2018.

Satterfield, Shirley, Educator, and Historian of the African-American community in Princeton, New Jersey, August 16 and September 26, 2017.

programs

Commencement Program. Rutgers College, New Brunswick, NJ, June 10th, 1919.

Robeson, Paul and Lawrence Brown and Bruno Raikin. August 10, 1958.

robeson's music

discography

A Lonesome Road. Paul Robeson. Academy Sound and Vision, 1966, Chapell
    Music, United Kingdom. CD AJA 5027, 1984. Produced by Kevin Daly.
    Transferred from 78s by Robert Parker/Vintage Productions.

On My Journey: Paul Robeson's Independent Recordings. Smithsonian National
    Museum of African American History and Culture, Legacy Recording,
    2007.

Robeson, Paul Live at Carnegie Hall: The Historic May 9. 1958 Concert. Vanguard
    Records, 1987.

Robeson, Paul. *Negro Spirituals (And More).* Roots Collection Vo. 10. IODA,
    2009, 2009 Discmedi S.A.

Robeson, Paul. *Songs of Free Men.* Lawrence Brown, piano. Columbia Concert
    Orchestra. Sony Music Entertainment, 1997.

Robeson, Paul. *The Original Recording of Ballad for Americans.* Alan Booth
    and Wingreen, Harriet, piano. Chorus and orchestra conducted by Milt
    Okum. Compact disc by James J. Frey. Prior release dates: 1958, 1963,
    1965. Copyright: 1989, 1967, 1965, Vanguard Records, a Welk Record
    Group Co.

video

Batten, Tony, executive producer. *A Profile of Paul Robeson.* Greater Washington
    Educational Telecommunications Association, 1975. Courtesy of Kit
    Parker Films, Carmel Valley, CA.

Nobel, Gil, dir. *Paul Robeson: A Biography. The Tallest Tree in Our Forest.* Canada:
    Black Cinema. Cascadia Entertainment, 1977.

Paul Robeson: Here I Stand. American Masters. WinStar TV & Video, 1999.

Paul Robeson: Portraits of the Artist: The Emperor Jones; Paul Robeson: Tribute to
    and Artist; Body and Soul; Borderline; Sanders of the River; Jericho; The Proud
    Valley; Native Land. The Criterion Collection.

Robeson, Paul, and Earl Robinson. *Bridge Across the Ocean*. (n.d.).

Show Boat, 1936. (16-mm movie; also on DVD).

Turell, Saul J., dir., writer. *Paul Robeson: A Tribute to an Artist*. The Paul Robeson Archives. Janus Films, October 1979.

walking tour of robeson sites in harlem

Alpha Phi Delta House, West 155th St.

Benta's Funeral Home, 630 St. Nicholas Avenue at 141st St.

Harlem YMCA, 180 West 135th St.

Mother A.M.E. Zion Church, 140–6 West 137th St.

New York Public Library, Schomburg Center for Research in Black Culture,
    515 Lenox Ave. (Malcolm X Blvd.) at 135th St.

residences

555 Edgecombe Avenue (co-named Paul Robeson Blvd.) at West 160th St.
    (Sugar Hill). Designated a National Historic Landmark; renamed
    The Paul Robeson Residence.

321 West 138th St., first home of Paul and Eslanda Robeson

16 Jumel Terrace, last home of Paul and Eslanda Robeson

source notes

Big Sea = The Big Sea, An Autobiography

Duberman = Paul Robeson: A Biography

Robeson Speaks = Paul Robeson Speaks: Writings, Speeches, and Interviews, 1918–1974

Undiscovered Robeson, 1898–1939 = The Undiscovered Paul Robeson: An Artist's Journey, 1898–1939

Undiscovered Robeson, 1939–1976 = The Undiscovered Paul Robeson: Quest for Freedom, 1939–1976

preface

"I did not . . .": Neruda, Pablo. Let the Rail Splitter Awake and Other Poems. New York: International Publishers, 1970, 1988, p. 37.

a note on terms used in this book

"I am a Negro": Robeson, quoted in Here I Stand.

"The origin of . . .": Robeson, quoted in Robeson Speaks, p. 88.

"Negro spirituals": Robeson, p. 73, "The Source of Negro Spirituals" (from Robeson Speaks).

"Negro American folk music": Robeson, 129 (from Robeson Speaks).

personal note

"domestic arrest": Duberman, p. 399.

"I am not being . . .": Robeson, quoted in Robeson, Paul Jr., p. 251 (from Undiscovered Robeson, 1939–1976).

chapter 1

"music event . . .": Broun's son, quoted in Duberman, p. 79.

"paralyzed with . . .": Davenport, quoted in Duberman, p. 80.

"It was really . . .": Robeson, p. 74 (from Robeson Speaks).

"The liberation theme . . .": Robeson, quoted in *Robeson Speaks*, p. 74.

"Go Down, Moses . . .": from "Go Down, Moses," African-American spiritual.

"Brown guided me . . .": Robeson, quoted in Duberman, p. 79.

"monotonous and uninteresting": Robeson, Eslanda, quoted in Duberman, p. 79.

"a perfect combination": Robeson, Eslanda, quoted in Duberman, p. 78.

"as if we were . . .": Robeson, quoted in Duberman, p. 79.

"With all my strength . . .": Davenport, quoted in Duberman, p. 80.

"*When Israel was . . .*": from "Go Down, Moses," African-American spiritual.

"carry him . . .": speaker, quoted in Duberman, p. 81.

"unconsciously . . .": Robeson, quoted in Duberman, p. 81.

"Everybody was . . .": Duberman, p. 80.

"By 'n' by . . .": from "By 'n' By," African-American spiritual.

"simply, unaffectedly, and beautifully. . .": Robeson, Eslanda, quoted in Lubasch, p. 42.

"Water boy . . .": from "Water Boy," African-American spiritual.

"Oh yes . . .": CD, Paul Robeson, Negro Spirituals (And More), Gospel 2, IODA.

"And the walls . . .": from "Joshua Fit the Battle of Jericho," African-American spiritual.

"It will . . .": quoted in *Paul Robeson, Negro*, p. 108.

"Paul Robeson's . . .": *New York World*, quoted in Lubasch, p. 42.

"May I tell you . . .": Du Bois, quoted in Duberman, p. 81.

"I couldn't possibly . . .": Robeson, quoted in Duberman, p. 81.

"Every time I appear . . .": Robeson, quoted in Duberman, p. 80.

chapter 2

"The glory of my . . .": Robeson, p. 6 (from *Here I Stand*).

"*No more auction block . . .*": from "Many Thousand Gone," African-American spiritual.

"greatest . . . a deep, sonorous . . .": Robeson p. 9 (from *Here I Stand*).

"voice going down . . .": Robeson, quoted in Duberman, p. 10.

"Almost every Negro . . .": Robeson, p. 260 (from *Robeson Speaks*).

"was always locked . . .": Leonard Rivers, quoted by Deborah Yaffe, "Across Nassau Street," *Princeton Alumni Weekly*, April 26, 2017, p. 24.

"colored": Robeson, Paul Jr., p. 5 (from *Undiscovered Robeson, 1898–1939*).

"the defender of justice": congregant, quoted in Duberman, p. 6.

"shack . . . so bad . . .": Robeson, quoted in Boyle & Bunie, p. 21.

"He was still . . .": Robeson, Paul, Jr., p. 6 (from *Undiscovered Robeson, 1898–1939*).

"little guide and inseparable": Robeson family friend, quoted in Boyle & Bunie, p. 23.

"I remember her . . .": Robeson, p. 7 (from *Here I Stand*).

"There must have . . .": Robeson, quoted in Duberman, p. 9.

"was crying too . . .": Abel, quoted in Boyle & Bunie, p. 148.

chapter 3

"During many of his . . .": Robeson, p. 9 (from *Here I Stand*).

"I remember the cornmeal . . .": Robeson, quoted in Brown, p. 31.

"I got plenty of . . .": Robeson, quoted in Boyle & Bunie, pp. 23–24.

"a warmth of song . . . spirituals." Robeson, quoted in Robeson, Paul Jr., pp. 8–9 (from *Undiscovered Robeson, 1898–1939*).

"*Nobody knows* . . .": from "Nobody Knows the Trouble I've Seen," African-American spiritual.

"*I got a home* . . .": from "I Got a Home in That Rock," African-American spiritual.

"I admired this rough . . .": Robeson, p. 12 (from *Here I Stand*).

"*Dee-ee-eep river* . . .": from "Deep River," African-American spiritual.

"Pop was pleased . . .": Robeson, p. 18 (from *Here I Stand*).

"When Paul cut loose . . .": Brown, quoted in Brown, p. 49.

"chording up . . .": Ben Robeson, quoted in Duberman, p. 14.

"Wait a minute . . .": Ben Robeson, quoted in Robeson, Paul Jr., p. 14 (from *Undiscovered Robeson, 1898–1939*).

"You can sing!": Robeson, Bill, quoted in Duberman, p. 14.

"making stupid jokes": Robeson, quoted in Duberman, p. 14.

"talent": Duberman, p. 14.

"good at stopping a man": speaker, quoted in Duberman, p. 16.

"sweetness and modesty": high school classmates, quoted in Duberman, p. 12.

"Nervous and . . . acting again": Robeson, p. 19 (from *Here I Stand*).

"and proved a huge hit . . .": Duberman, p. 13.

"shied away . . . social life . . . dance with me": Robeson, quoted in Robeson, Paul Jr., p. 14. (from *Undiscovered Robeson, 1898–1939*).

"All of us were . . .": Kershaw, quoted in Brown, p. 50.

"Well, I was . . . *that* good!": Duberman, p. 13.

"Singer? No . . . . a career": Robeson, p. 24 (from *Here I Stand*).

"Warmth of song . . . . their harmonies": Robeson, quoted in Robeson, Paul Jr., p. 9 (from *Undiscovered Robeson, 1898–1939*).

chapter 4

"I don't want . . . made easy": Robeson, quoted in Duberman, p. 17.

"Credit to His Race": Brown, p. 65.

"Be a credit . . . ": Watterson, p. 81.

"the Negro problem": W. E. B. Du Bois quoted in Kendi, Ibram X. *Stamped From the Beginning*. New York: National Books, 2016, p. 329.

"Here was a decisive . . .": Robeson, p. 25 (from *Here I Stand*).

"an almost unexplainable . . .": Robeson, quoted in Boyle & Bunie, p. 55.

"stared at him . . .": Robeson, Paul Jr., p. 20 (from *Undiscovered Robeson, 1898–1939*).

"friendly manner . . . expressed anger": Robeson, Paul Jr., p. 21 (from *Undiscovered Robeson, 1898–1939*).

"sings" and "Gopher Dust": Duberman, p. 574.

"natural singer . . .": Robeson, Paul Jr., p. 21 (from *Undiscovered Robeson, 1898–1939*).

"their": Robeson, quoted in Brown, p. 60.

"They didn't . . . any more": Robeson, quoted in Brown, p. 60.

"I was the representative . . .": Robeson, quoted in Brown, p. 61.

"Kid, if you want . . .": Robeson, Bill, quoted in Brown, p. 61.

"That's when . . . kill him . . . the varsity": Robeson, quoted in Brown, p. 61.

"acting right": Brown, p. 69.

"I feel sorry . . .": Wittpenn, quoted in Boyle & Bunie, p. 54.

"I used to . . . sing again": Robeson, quoted in Duberman, p. 24.

"They preferred . . . Paul's singing": Neuschafer, quoted in Brown, p. 71.

"Before the service . . .": Robeson, quoted in Boyle & Bunie, p. 57.

"On my journey . . .": from "On My Journey, Mount Zion," African-American spiritual.

"Everybody knew . . . each other": Robeson, quoted in Brown, p. 67.

"keeping company": Brown, p. 67.

"Negro girls . . . *brown* eyes": Neale, quoted in Boyle & Bunie, p. 63.

"football genius . . . this season": sportswriters, quoted in Duberman, p. 22.

"a veritable superman": Camp, quoted in Duberman, p. 22.

"These one-man . . .": Robeson, quoted in Robeson, Paul Jr., p. 32 (from *Undiscovered Robeson, 1898–1939*).

chapter 5

"I want you to win": William Robeson, quoted in Boyle & Bunie, p. 69.

"Paul stood there . . .": Robeson friend, quoted in Duberman, p. 25.

"zeal . . . his people": Duberman, p. 30.

"a destiny to fulfill . . .": Robeson, Paul Jr., p. 32 (from *Undiscovered Robeson, 1898–1939*).

"lovingly prepared . . .": Robeson, Paul Jr., p. 32 (from *Undiscovered Robeson, 1898–1939*).

"There's a man": from "There's a Man Going Around Taking Names," African-American spiritual.

"I was not sure . . .": Neale, quoted in Duberman, p. 29.

"Who would ever . . .": friends of Neale, quoted in Duberman, p. 29.

"he was a man . . .": Neale, quoted in Paul Robeson, Paul Jr., p. 46 (from *Undiscovered Robeson, 1898–1939*).

"Gerry—she was just . . . for me": Robeson, quoted in Brown, p. 67.

"We of this less. . . . opportunities for all.": Robeson, quoted in Duberman, pp. 26–27.

"an era when . . .": Robeson, Paul Jr., p. 36 (from *Undiscovered Robeson, 1898–1939*).

"the cultured . . .": Chinn, quoted in Duberman, p. 33.

"Oh, Danny boy . . .": from "Danny Boy," Irish melody.

chapter 6

"Noisy and childish": Robeson, quoted in Boyle & Bunie, p. 82.

"I really didn't know . . .": Robeson, quoted in Brown, p. 114.

"A Man Was . . .": Holland Cotter, "A Memorial to the Lingering of Lynching."
     The New York Times, June 1, 2018, p. AR1.

"charmed the crowd": speaker, quoted in Boyle & Bunie, p. 83.

"was deep into . . .": Douglas, quoted in Robeson, Paul Jr., p. 50 (from
     Undiscovered Robeson, 1898–1939).

"Then we discovered . . .": Higgins, quoted in Brown, p. 111.

"great cavern": Murray, quoted in Duberman, p. 34.

"Paul was making . . . engaging smile": Robeson, Eslanda, quoted in Robeson,
     Paul Jr., p. 46 (from *Undiscovered Robeson, 1898–1939*).

"He was . . . into song": Robeson, Eslanda, p. 70.

"When she [Essie] saw . . .": friend of Eslanda Robeson, quoted in Boyle
     & Bunie, p. 88.

"Harlem's darling": Robeson, Eslanda, quoted in Ransby, p. 29.

"a campaign to win . . . something of him": Robeson, Eslanda, quoted in Boyle
     & Bunie, p. 89.

"dragged him in . . .": Robeson, quoted in Duberman, p. 43.

"How I happened . . .": Robeson, quoted in Boyle & Bunie, p. 89.

"far too dark": Goode, quoted in Paul Robeson Jr., p. 50 (from *Undiscovered
     Robeson, 1898–1939*).

"The New Negro . . .": Goode, quoted in Ransby, p. 25.

"lacked the ambition . . .": Robeson, Paul Jr., p. 50 (from *Undiscovered Robeson,
     1898–1939*).

"aristocratic": Robeson, Paul Jr., p. 50 (from *Undiscovered Robeson, 1898–1939*).

"He suggested that . . .": Robeson, Eslanda, quoted in Duberman, p. 41.

"unsupportive": Robeson, Paul Jr., p. 53 (from *Undiscovered Robeson, 1898–1939*).

"I knew little . . .": Robeson, quoted in Duberman, p. 43.

"stage presence": press report, Duberman, p. 44.

"rich, mellow": press report, quoted in Duberman, p. 43.

"that he belonged . . .": Duberman, p. 44.

"I never in my life": Woollcott, quoted in Duberman, p. 44.

"*What* have you . . . . fairly famous": Robeson, quoted in Robeson, Paul Jr.,
    p. 57 (from *Undiscovered Robeson, 1898–1939*).

"It never occurred . . .": Robeson, Eslanda, quoted in Robeson, Paul Jr., p. 56
    (from *Undiscovered Robeson, 1898–1939*).

"Brother, you're . . .": Robeson, quoted in Robeson, Paul Jr., p. 58 (from
    Undiscovered Robeson, 1898–1939).

"He was astonished": Paul Robeson Jr., p. 58 (from *Undiscovered Robeson,
    1898–1939*).

"closed her eyes . . .": Duberman, p. 44.

"That boy will bear. . . some personality!": Blake, quoted in Duberman, p. 45.

"set her mind and heart": Duberman, p. 44.

"He didn't want . . . to the top": Robeson, Eslanda, quoted in Robeson, Paul
    Jr., p. 56 (from *Undiscovered Robeson, 1898–1939*).

"*We are climbing* . . .": from "Jacob's Ladder," African-American spiritual.

chapter 7

"I had never. . . . I had left": Seton, p. 9.

"We don't allow. . .": Williams, quoted in Duberman, p. 34.

"friendly welcome . . . scholar. . . . at home": Robeson, pp. 32–33 (from *Here
    I Stand*).

"The play is . . .": Robeson, quoted in Robeson, Paul Jr., p. 62 (from
    Undiscovered Robeson, 1898–1939).

"To be truthful . . .": Duberman, p. 48.

"Mrs. Campbell doesn't . . .": Robeson, quoted in Robeson, Paul Jr., p. 63 (from
    Undiscovered Robeson, 1898–1939).

"I think that . . . , come back": Robeson, quoted in Robeson, Paul Jr. pp. 63–64
    (from *Undiscovered Robeson, 1898–1939*).

"digs": Seton, p. 11.

"labouring folk . . . friendliness": Seton, p. 12.

"Sing it louder . . .": Campbell, quoted in Boyle & Bunie, p. 107.

"I was merely singing . . .": Robeson, quoted in Seton, p. 13.

"The audiences loved . . .": Robeson, quoted in Brown, p. 120.

"turned into dramatic action": Robeson, quoted in Boyle & Bunie, p. 107.

"It is the consensus. . . . more, more": Robeson, quoted in Robeson, Paul Jr., p. 64 (from *Undiscovered Robeson, 1898–1939*).

"real artist . . . Othello": Campbell, quoted in Duberman, p. 50.

"So anxious . . . help me.": Robeson, quoted in Duberman, p. 50.

"I don't want . . .": Robeson, quoted in Robeson, Paul Jr., p. 63 (from *Undiscovered Robeson, 1898–1939*).

"London was the center . . . ever since": Robeson, p. 33 (from *Here I Stand*).

"flat": Seton, p. 10.

"*Steal away . . .*": from "Steal Away," African-American spiritual.

"It was this musician . . .": Robeson, quoted in Brown, p. 123.

"just for . . . . ever work together": Seton, p. 10.

"Cheerio, old chap": Brown, quoted in Brown, p. 122.

"dominating personality . . .": theater critic, quoted in Duberman, p. 50.

"You'll know what . . .": Robeson, quoted in Robeson, Paul Jr., p. 64 (from *Undiscovered Robeson, 1898–1939*).

"All my questions. . . . absolutely offguard" Robeson, quoted in Duberman, p. 51.

"I cried and cried . . . together": Robeson, quoted in Duberman, p. 51.

chapter 8

"His heart was . . .": classmate, quoted in Boyle & Bunie, p. 113.

"He felt he . . .": Woollcott, quoted in Robeson, Paul Jr., p. 70 (from *Undiscovered Robeson, 1898–1939*).

"He idled away . . .": Robeson, Eslanda, p. 73.

"Something will turn up": Robeson, quoted in Duberman, p. 55.

"inner revelation": Robeson, Ben, quoted in Duberman, p. 54.

"When important cases . . . . case": Patterson, quoted in Boyle & Bunie, p. 112.

"I don't even think . . .": Patterson, quoted in Boyle & Bunie, p. 113.

"This was an . . .": Robeson, Eslanda, p. 73.

"No one could . . .": Robeson, Eslanda, p. 74.

"I never take . . .": stenographer, quoted in Duberman, p. 55.

"If I'm going . . .": Robeson, quoted in Boyle & Bunie, p. 114.

"any profession where . . .": Robeson, quoted in Duberman, p. 55.

"temperamentally unsuited . . .": Salemme, quoted in Boyle & Bunie, p. 114.

"and more . . .": Robeson, Paul Jr., p. 77 (from *Undiscovered Robeson, 1898–1939*).

"Something will . . .": Robeson, quoted in Robeson, Eslanda, p. 75.

"How proud I . . .": Robeson, quoted in Boyle & Bunie, p. 112.

"All I remember . . . personality": Bess Rockmore, quoted in Duberman, p. 55.

"he liked to sing . . .": Robeson, Paul Jr., p. 74 (from *Undiscovered Robeson, 1898–1939*).

"The gospel train's a comin'. . .": from "The Gospel Train," African-American spiritual.

"strapping man . . .": *Philadelphia Record* critic, quoted in Lubasch, p. 32.

"extremely interesting": *Philadelphia Record* critic, quoted in Duberman, p. 57.

"Riots Feared from . . .": New York *American*, quoted in Duberman, p. 57.

"For days and nights . . .": Duberman, p. 59.

"feel his way": Robeson, Eslanda, quoted in Duberman, p. 60.

"I can't tell . . . move": Light, quoted in Duberman, p. 60.

"I am . . .": Robeson, quoted in Duberman, p. 60.

"Then just take . . .": Light, quoted in Duberman, p. 60.

"stiff, nervous": Robeson, Eslanda, quoted in Robeson, Paul Jr., p. 76 (from *Undiscovered Robeson, 1898–1939*).

"easy and natural": Robeson, Eslanda, quoted in Robeson, Paul Jr., p. 76 (from *Undiscovered Robeson, 1898–1939*).

"Paul was superb . . . defeaning": Robeson, Eslanda, quoted in Robeson, Paul Jr., p. 76 (from *Undiscovered Robeson, 1898–1939*).

"Robeson held his . . ." *New York Telegram*, quoted in Robeson, Paul Jr., p. 76 (from *Undiscovered Robeson, 1898–1939*).

"hard worker . . . studied intensively": Gilpin, quoted in Robeson, Paul Jr., p. 76 (from *Undiscovered Robeson, 1898–1939*).

"When I went . . .": Robeson, quoted in Duberman, p. 63.

"seemed . . . applause": Robeson, Eslanda, quoted in Robeson, Paul Jr., p. 77 (from *Undiscovered Robeson, 1898–1939*).

"genius" and "great actor": *New York World*, quoted in Duberman, p. 64.

"a hard play . . . entertainment": Budd, quoted in Duberman, p. 65.

"The Ku Klux Klan . . .": NAACP reviewer, quoted in Duberman, p. 65.

"I would have more. . . .": Robeson, quoted in Duberman, p. 67.

"In the law . . .": Robeson, quoted in Lubasch, p. 37.

chapter 9

"race films": Lane, on producer Oscar Micheaux (from *Black Broadway*). p. 55.

"I realized even . . .": Robeson, quoted in Boyle & Bunie, p. 132.

"Paul's voice was . . .": Hayes, George, quoted in Boyle & Bunie, p. 143.

"He had this presence . . .": Salemme, quoted in Duberman, p. 68.

"Just think of . . .": Salemme, quoted in Duberman, p. 69.

"I enjoy singing . . .": Robeson, quoted in Robeson, Eslanda, p. 98.

"If I can . . .": Robeson, quoted in Robeson, Eslanda, pp. 97–98.

"Negro Spiritual": Duberman, image #22.

"I went to see . . .": Robeson, quoted in Duberman, p. 72.

"We wanted supper . . . discarded": White, quoted in Lubasch, p. 37.

"fear of insult": Lubasch, p. 37.

"It is through . . .": Robeson, quoted in Robeson, Paul Jr., p. 88 (from *Undiscovered Robeson, 1898–1939*).

"The 1920s were. . . .": Hughes, Langston. p. 223 (from *The Big Sea*).

"white people began to . . .": Hughes, Langston. p. 224 (from *The Big Sea*).

"It was a . . .": Hughes, p. 227 (from *The Big Sea*).

"singing spirituals . . .": Van Vechten, quoted in Duberman, p. 73.

"There, standing on . . . ." and "spontaneous": Brown, quoted in Seton, p. 35.

"the most humble . . . beauty": Robeson, quoted in Robeson, Paul Jr., p. 87 (from *Undiscovered Robeson, 1898–1939*).

"Why don't you . . .": Light, quoted in Seton, p. 35.

"threshed out . . .": Brown, quoted in Lubasch, p. 39.

"begged for . . .": Robeson, Eslanda, quoted in Lubasch, p. 40.

"We all promoted . . .": Abel, Walter, quoted in Boyle & Bunie, p. 143.

"We chose what . . .": Brown, quoted in Lubasch, p. 41.

"all-Negro music": Robeson, Eslanda, p. 101.

"They were both . . .": Robeson, Eslanda, quoted in Robeson, Paul Jr., p. 87 (from *Undiscovered Robeson, 1898–1939*).

"When the boys appeared . . .": Robeson, Paul Jr., p. 87 (from *Undiscovered Robeson, 1898–1939*).

"When Israel . . .": from "Go Down Moses," African American spiritual.

"For I hope . . .": from "I Don't Feel No Ways Tired," African-American spiritual.

"I's a sighin' . . .": from "L'il Gal," African-American spiritual.

"If I can . . .": Robeson, quoted in Robeson, Eslanda, p. 97.

"After each number . . .": Robeson, Eslanda, quoted in Lubasch, p. 42.

"The boys got curtain . . .": Robeson, Eslanda, Robeson, Paul Jr., p. 87 (from
      Undiscovered Robeson, 1898–1939).

"I simply couldn't . . . meaning": Robeson, p. 77 (from *Robeson Speaks*).

chapter 10

"nice cozy place": Robeson, Eslanda, quoted in Duberman, p. 87.

"warm and friendly . . .": Robeson, Eslanda, quoted in Duberman, p. 87.

"felt even more . . .": Robeson, Eslanda, p. 110.

"without fear of the . . .": Robeson, Eslanda, pp. 110–111.

"wonderful voice": Boyle & Bunie, p. 162.

"astonishing emotional powers": Boyle & Bunie, p. 162.

"I am thrilled . . . has the voice": Robeson, quoted in Boyle & Bunie, p. 162.

"Mr. Robeson": Boyle & Bunie, p. 162.

"Why No! . . . black races": Robeson, quoted in Boyle & Bunie, pp. 162–163.

"made up his mind . . .": Robeson, Eslanda, p. 123.

"I have just . . .": Robeson, Eslanda, p. 124.

"with every courtesy": Robeson, Eslanda, quoted in Duberman, p. 100.

"I feel awful . . .": Robeson, quoted in Robeson, Eslanda, p. 127.

"I think you ought . . .": Brown, quoted in Robeson, Eslanda, p. 127.

"was so . . . nervousness": Robeson, Eslanda, *Paul Robeson, Negro*, p. 127–128.

"I've married the . . .": Robeson, Eslanda, p. 130.

"when Robeson sings . . .": Woollcott, quoted in Boyle & Bunie, p. 178.

"I can make . . .": Robeson, quoted in Boyle & Bunie, p. 179.

"The melody . . . called inspiration.": Kern, quoted in Decker, p. 39.

"Robeson recital": Decker, p. 49.

"White folks . . .": Wilkins, quoted in Duberman, pp. 105–106.

"mixed feelings": Robeson, Eslanda, quoted in Duberman, p. 106.

"You know you're . . .": Robeson, quoted in Robeson, Eslanda, p. 136.

"I'll take a chance . . .": Robeson, Eslanda, p. 136.

"art": Lubasch, p. 49.

"I feel that . . .": Lubasch, p. 49.

"So hard to . . .": Robeson, quoted in Robeson, Paul Jr., p. 143 (from
    Undiscovered Robeson, 1898–1939).

"He was an . . . startling": Robeson, Eslanda, p. 137.

"How can that . . .": Robeson, quoted in Robeson, Paul Jr., p. 145 (from
    Undiscovered Robeson, 1898–1939).

"Just you wait . . .": Robeson, quoted in Robeson, Paul Jr., p. 148 (from
    Undiscovered Robeson, 1898–1939).

"My God, Paul . . .": Kern, quoted in Lubasch, p. 53.

"Paul just walked up . . .": cast member, quoted in Lubasch, p. 53.

chapter 11

"so trying . . . a 'baby'": Robeson, quoted in Duberman, p. 114.

"remained superb": *Observer* critic, quoted in Duberman, p. 114.

"inept and clumsy": *Sunday Times* critic, quoted in Duberman, p. 114.

"good-natured, lolling . . .": *Amsterdam News* critic, quoted in Duberman,
    p. 114.

"servant class": Robeson, p. 10 (from *Here I Stand*).

"*You and me . . .*": from "Ol' Man River," Kern, Jerome.

"People went . . . a knot. . . . like a child": actors, quoted in Boyle & Bunie,
    p. 192.

"Grandma Goode was . . .": Robeson, Paul Jr., p. 148 (from *Undiscovered
    Robeson, 1898–1939*).

"Brown worked incessantly. . . . pitch": Seton, pp. 40–41.

"extremely sensitive to . . .": Seton, p. 41.

"Their text is . . . miracle happening": Robeson, pp. 73–74 (from *Robeson
    Speaks*).

"One of the . . .": Robeson p. 75 (from *Robeson Speaks*).

"know the strong . . .": Robeson, quoted in Robeson, Eslanda, p. 97.

"*Water boy . . .*": from "Water Boy," African-American spiritual.

"Paul took the . . .": Robeson, Eslanda, quoted in Duberman, p. 115.

"sat there in a trance": *Daily Express* critic, quoted in Decker, *Show Boat*, p. 137.

"*Ezekiel saw . . .*": from "Ezekiel Saw the Wheel," African-American spiritual.

"alight and aflame. . . . intensity": Robeson, Eslanda, p. 140.

"It looks as. . . . jugs": Robeson, Eslanda, quoted in Duberman, p. 115.

"bored to death . . .": Robeson, quoted in Duberman, p. 120.

"fantastic religiousness": Budapest reporters, Boyle & Bunie, p. 209.

"Slav peasant music. . . . yoke": Robeson, quoted in Duberman, p. 129.

"the largest crowd . . . 'Robey'": unidentified speaker, quoted in Duberman, p. 125.

"cataclysmic events. . . . life": Robeson, Paul Jr., p. 163 (from *Undiscovered Robeson, 1898–1939*).

"I don't know . . . this power. . . . I'll win": Robeson, quoted in Lubasch, p. 58.

chapter 12

"Negro": Robeson, quoted in Duberman, p. 137.

"When you shall . . .": Shakespeare, William, *Othello*, Act V, Scene II., p. 153.

"I feel. . . . of jealousy": Robeson, quoted in Seton, p. 53.

"When a negro . . . culmination": Robeson, p. 67 (from *Robeson Speaks*).

"I think I'll . . . at it.": Robeson, quoted in Robeson, Eslanda, pp. 155–156.

"I know you . . .": Robeson, Eslanda, p. 156.

"All right . . .": Robeson, quoted in Robeson, Eslanda, p. 156.

"Here is . . . work very hard . . . the fact . . . white society": Robeson (from Batten, *A Profile of Paul Robeson*).

"moving like . . .": Robeson, quoted in Seton, p. 54.

"Nellie doesn't . . . is lost": Robeson, Eslanda, quoted in Duberman, p. 134.

"Mr. Robeson, there are . . .": Van Volkenburg, Nellie, quoted in Duberman, p. 134.

"For us young people . . . ": Ashcroft, quoted in Duberman, p. 134.

"How could one . . . inevitable": Ashcroft, quoted in Duberman, p. 140.

"wild with . . . a patch": Robeson, Eslanda, quoted in Duberman, p. 136.

"started off . . .": Robeson, quoted in Duberman, p. 136.

"frenzy of . . .": *New York Times*, quoted in Lubasch, p. 62.

"Robeson! Robeson! . . .": Seton, p. 54.

"I took the part . . .": Robeson, quoted in Seton, p. 54.

"magnificent . . . disappointing . . . soldier": critics, quoted in Duberman, p. 137.

"glowing notices": Lubasch, p. 62.

"They caught the . . .": Robeson, Eslanda, quoted in Duberman, p. 136.

"fled like . . .": actor, quoted in Duberman, p. 138.

"He has been working . . .": Robeson, Eslanda, quoted in Duberman, p. 137.

"liberating . . . free": Robeson, quoted in Duberman, p. 137.

"by a coloured . . . Paul Robeson": Ashcroft, quoted in Duberman, p. 135.

"A rotten parent . . . dishonest artist": Duberman, p. 140.

"He must have . . . there was one": Robeson, Eslanda, quoted in Duberman, p. 140.

"I must have . . . interested . . . come out right": Robeson, quoted in Duberman, pp. 141–142.

"secret, mean, low": Robeson, Eslanda, quoted in Duberman, p. 143.

chapter 13

"Paul saw far . . .": Robeson, Eslanda, p. 157.

"At first, naturally . . . he wants": Robeson, Eslanda, quoted in Duberman, p. 144.

"I do so . . .": Robeson, Eslanda, quoted in Duberman, p. 145.

"art songs": critic, quoted in Duberman, p. 146.

"more intelligent . . . their race": newspaper reports, quoted in Duberman, p. 146.

"something beneath their . . .": newspaper reports, quoted in Duberman, p. 146.

"ought to do as many . . .": Roberson in an interview with Roy Wilkins, quoted in Duberman, p. 146.

"Nothing was going . . .": Brown, quoted in Duberman, p. 146.

"Is he fed up . . . his work?": Robeson, Eslanda, quoted in Duberman, p. 146.

"What I really need . . .": Robeson, quoted in Duberman, p. 147.

"The rehearsals nearly . . . physical strength": Robeson, quoted in Duberman, p. 148.

"He is using much . . . strain it": Robeson, Eslanda, quoted in Duberman, p. 148.

"magnificent": quoted in Duberman, p. 149.

"no voice at all": Robeson, Eslanda, quoted in Duberman, p. 149.

"There is a . . .": Robeson, quoted in Robeson, Paul Jr., p. 185 (from *Undiscovered Robeson, 1898–1939*).

"The Captive": Boyle & Bunie, p. 251.

"Paul is behaving. . . . for him": Robeson, Eslanda, quoted in Duberman, p. 151.

"He wanted to. . . .": Robeson, Paul Jr., p. 186 (from *Undiscovered Robeson, 1898–1939*).

"played together happily": Robeson, Paul Jr., p. 190 (from *Undiscovered Robeson, 1898–1939*).

"There's no hidin' . . .": from "There's No Hidin' Place Down There," African-American spiritual.

"no one . . . back": Ferber, quoted in Boyle & Bunie, p. 253.

"NOMORESEATS": Boyle & Bunie, p. 253.

"In all my years . . . or the opera": Ferber, quoted in Boyle & Bunie, p. 253.

"they called him . . .": quoted in Lubasch, p. 69.

"celestial": *New York Herald Tribune,* quoted in Boyle & Bunie, p. 253.

"Mr. Robeson has . . .": *New York Times*, quoted in Lubasch, p. 69.

"not only an . . . friend": Pobeson, quoted in Robeson, Paul Jr., p. 200 (from *Undiscovered Robeson, 1898–1939*). "This country is . . .": Robeson, quoted in Robeson, Paul Jr., p. 194 (from *Undiscovered Robeson, 1898–1939*).

"the greatest. . . . prejudice . . . self-respect": Robeson, quoted in Robeson, Paul Jr., p. 194 (from *Undiscovered Robeson, 1898–1939*).

"Paul and I are . . .": Robeson, Eslanda, quoted in Duberman, p. 162.

"the beginning of . . .": Robeson, Eslanda, quoted in Duberman, p. 164.

"I enjoyed long . . .": Robeson, Paul Jr., p. 198 (from *Undiscovered Robeson, 1898–1939*).

chapter 14

"as a professional team": Robeson, Paul Jr., p. 198 (from *Undiscovered Robeson, 1898–1939*).

"Am terribly happy . . .": Robeson, quoted in Duberman, p. 166.

"I am proud. . . .": Robeson, quoted in Duberman, p. 169.

"I am learning . . .": Robeson, quoted in Robeson, Paul Jr., pp. 208–209 (from *Undiscovered Robeson, 1898–1939*).

"Negro English . . . homecoming": Robeson, quoted in Duberman, p. 170.

"People almost fought . . .": Seton, p. 64.

"A perfect dramatic partnership": *Observer*, quoted in Duberman, p. 167.

"Flora Robson makes . . .": *News-Chronicle*, quoted in Robeson, Paul Jr., p. 205
(from *Undiscovered Robeson, 1898–1939*).

"a long way . . .": Robeson, Paul Jr., p. 205 (from *Undiscovered Robeson,
1898–1939*).

"My whole social. . . . about Socialism": Robeson, quoted in Lubasch, p. 56.

"I'm an artist. . . .": Seton, p. 68.

"If I allow . . .": hotel manager, quoted in Boyle & Bunie, p. 276.

"defiance mixed with fear": Robeson, Paul Jr., p. 207 (from *Undiscovered
Robeson, 1898–1939*).

"the plantation type . . .": Robeson, quoted in Robeson, Paul Jr., p. 208 (from
Undiscovered Robeson, 1898–1939).

"human stories": Robeson, quoted in Duberman, p. 169.

"O'Neill does not. . . . morons": Rogers, Joel, quoted in Boyle & Bunie, p. 282.

"Coming from the . . .": Robeson, quoted in Duberman, p. 168.

"common humanity": Robeson, quoted in Lubasch, p. 77.

"I have had . . .": Gershwin, quoted in Robeson, Paul Jr., p. 215 (from
Undiscovered Robeson, 1898–1939).

"magnificent": Robeson, quoted in Duberman, p. 178.

"much more melody . . . heritage": Robeson, quoted in Duberman, p. 179.

"I spoke to . . .": Robeson, quoted in Seton, p. 78.

"For the first . . .": Robeson, quoted in Duberman, p. 179.

"I remember. . . . person": Robeson, Paul Jr., p. 212 (from *Undiscovered Robeson,
1898–1939*).

"I personally am . . .": Robeson, quoted in Duberman, p. 627.

"I hate the picture": Robeson, quoted in Duberman, p. 182.

"a grand insight . . ." *London Times*, quoted in Duberman, p. 180.

"Childlike and . . ." Robeson, quoted in Duberman, p. 180.

"Look, we have . . .": Duberman, p. 181.

"All money earned . . .": Robeson, quoted in Duberman, p. 627.

"It is not. . . . and sing": Robeson, pp. 92 and 94 (from *Robeson Speaks*).

chapter 15

"was proof of . . .": Robeson, Paul Jr., p. 213 (from *Undiscovered Robeson,
1898–1939*).

"nightmare": Robeson, Eslanda, quoted in Lubasch, p. 78.

"It was like . . .": Robeson, quoted in Brown, p. 125.

"Paul said he . . . brooding look": Seton, p. 82.

"I feel I need . . .": Robeson, quoted in Seton, p. 82.

"He strode . . . deliberation": Seton, p. 82.

"I thought you . . . my case . . . than necessary.": Robeson, quoted in Seton, p. 82.

"This is like . . . our heads": Robeson, quoted in Seton, p. 83.

"fear . . . fury": Seton, p. 83.

"They think you . . .": Robeson, quoted in Seton, p. 83.

"Get on!": Robeson, quoted in Seton, p. 84.

"I never understood . . .": Robeson, quoted in Seton, p. 84.

chapter 16

"I find it much . . . feelings": Robeson, p. 108 (from *Robeson Speaks*).

"I would like. . .": Robeson, quoted in Seton, p. 90.

"The Russians have . . .": Robeson, quoted in Boyle & Bunie, p. 303.

"dearest, beloved little. . .": Seton, p. 93.

"Meesseesseeppee": Robeson, Paul Jr., p. 221 (from *Undiscovered Robeson, 1898–1939*).

"Only that it . . . anywhere else": Robeson, pp. 94–95 (from *Robeson Speaks*).

"It is the government's . . .": Robeson, p. 95 (from *Robeson Speaks*).

"He was an . . .": Lubasch, "In Harlem With: Paul Robeson Jr.; Finding His Own Voice and Learning to Use It," *New York Times*, 1993.

"a new sense of purpose": Robeson, Paul Jr., p. 217 (from *Undiscovered Robeson, 1898–1939*).

"I made it . . . is the bunk . . . enough to eat": Robeson, p. 106 (from *Robeson Speaks*).

"black Grandfather Frost": Robeson, Paul Jr., p. 221 (from *Undiscovered Robeson, 1898–1939*).

"sincere friendliness": Robeson, quoted in Duberman, p. 189.

"I feel like . . .": Robeson, quoted in Seton, p. 95.

chapter 17

"Why, it's the . . .": Robeson, p. 105 (from *Robeson Speaks*).

"non-political": Robeson, quoted in Duberman, p. 190.

"Deep down inside . . .": Robeson, quoted in Duberman, p. 201.

"When I step . . . shack": Robeson, p. 119 (from *Robeson Speaks*).

"working in brick . . .": Robeson quoted in Stewart, *Paul Robeson: Artist and Citizen*, p. 180.

"I like singing. . . . sing": Robeson, p. 120 (from *Robeson Speaks*).

"When I sing . . . working-class": Robeson, p. 119 (from *Robeson Speaks*).

"All races all . . .": Robeson, quoted in Duberman, p. 202.

"After the greatest . . .": Brown, quoted in Lubasch, p. 75.

"I think my . . .": Robeson, quoted in Robeson, Paul Jr., p. 227 (from *Undiscovered Robeson, 1898–1939*).

"He chanted Yiddish . . .": Marshall, quoted in Boyle & Bunie, p. 311.

"I was tired. . . . white environment": Robeson, Paul Jr., pp. 232–233 (from *Undiscovered Robeson, 1898–1939*).

"We think the . . .": Robeson, Eslanda, quoted in Duberman, p. 195.

"in his soft . . .": Robeson, Paul Jr., p. 233 (from *Undiscovered Robeson, 1898–1939*).

"They tell me . . .": Robeson, Eslanda, quoted in Robeson, Paul Jr., p. 233 (from *Undiscovered Robeson, 1898–1939*).

"synching . . . intimate fashion": Robeson, Paul Jr., p. 234 (from *Undiscovered Robeson, 1898–1939*).

"opulent spectacular . . . magnificent in scope": critics, quoted in Boyle & Bunie, p. 336.

"experiment with . . .": Robeson, Paul Jr., p. 234 (from *Undiscovered Robeson, 1898–1939*).

"made good on . . . the household": Robeson, Paul Jr., p. 236 (from *Undiscovered Robeson, 1898–1939*).

"natives": Duberman, p. 207.

"thundering good": *Sunday Chronicle*, quoted in Lubasch, p. 89.

"South African Jim Crow": Robeson, p. 307 (from *Robeson Speaks*).

"Africa was opened . . .": Duberman, p. 203.

"*Look down* . . .": Shilkret Nathaniel and Austin, Gene, "Lonesome Road," 1927.

"Now was not . . .": Robeson, Paul Jr., p. 240 (from *Undiscovered Robeson, 1898–1939*).

"one of those . . .": Robeson, Eslanda, quoted in Lubasch, p. 89.

"steady, trustworthy . . .": Duberman, p. 208.

"Slav admiration": *Life* magazine, quoted in Robeson, Paul Jr., p. 280 (from *Undiscovered Robeson, 1898–1939*).

"I want to be . . .": Robeson, p. 88 (from *Robeson Speaks*).

"In my music . . .": Robeson, p. 91 (from *Robeson Speaks*).

"triumphant black hero": Robeson, Paul Jr., p. 281 (from *Undiscovered Robeson, 1898–1939*).

"It's the best. . . . wonderful place": Robeson, quoted in Duberman, p. 209.

"It's great fun . . .": Robeson, Eslanda, quoted in Robeson, Paul Jr., p. 282 (from *Undiscovered Robeson, 1898–1939*).

"almost crumbled . . .": Wilcoxon, quoted in Duberman, p. 209.

"spellbound—not moving . . . silently crying": Wilcoxon, quoted in Lubasch, p. 93.

"There were tears . . .": Wilcoxon, quoted in Duberman, p. 210.

chapter 18

"greatest cause": Robeson, quoted in Lubasch, p. 94.

"The cause of . . . events": Robeson, p. 117 (from *Robeson Speaks*).

"Fascism is no . . . alternative": Robeson, quoted in Lubasch, p. 94.

"This is our . . .": Robeson, quoted in Lubasch, p. 95.

"safe-conduct orders": Duberman, p. 215.

"It is not. . . . in the world": Robeson, quoted in Duberman, p. 216.

"We then went . . . River": Robeson, Eslanda, quoted in Lubasch, p. 96.

"*I gets weary . . .*": Kern, Jerome, and Oscar Hammerstein II, "Ol' Man River."

"lit up . . . drawing you . . . in": medical corps sergeant, quoted in Duberman, p. 218.

"which windows would . . .": Robeson, Paul Jr., p. 300 (from *Undiscovered Robeson, 1898–1939*).

"went wild with joy": soldiers, quoted in Boyle & Bunie, p. 383.

"a turning point" Robeson, quoted in Lubash, p. 98.

"To me Spain . . ." Boyle & Bunie, p. 385.

"This is OUR . . .": Robeson, quoted in Robeson, Paul Jr., p. 303 (from *Undiscovered Robeson, 1898–1939*).

chapter 19

"Robeson was not . . . party": Robeson acquaintances, quoted in Boyle & Bunie, p. 382.

"It is my . . . harm": Robeson's agent, quoted in Duberman, p. 222.

"*From border to . . .*": from "Border to Border,": popular Soviet song from the opera *Quiet Flows the Don*.

"a people's theatre": Duberman, p. 223.

"I've managed to . . .": Robeson, quoted in Lubasch, p. 99.

"stood with tears . . .": *Scotsman*, quoted in Seton, p. 115.

"soon had everyone laughing . . .": Empire Exhibition, "Paul Robeson the Attraction," *Scotsman*, Friday, Septmber 2, 1938.

"*Put on the skillet . . .*": from "Shortnin' Bread," plantation song.

"It was the . . . for the people": Brown, quoted in Seton, p. 115.

"dreadful things": Robeson, quoted in Duberman, p. 221.

"innocent people had . . . war": Robeson, quoted in Robeson, Paul Jr., p. 306 (from *Undiscovered Robeson, 1898–1939*).

"Gaining equality for . . . nationality": Robeson, quoted in Boyle & Bunie, p. 369.

"The politics threatened . . . a bit": Robeson's booking agent, quoted in Boyle & Bunie, p. 369.

"lonesome road": author quoting lyric from song.

"I myself can scarcely . . .": Roosevelt, Franklin, quoted in Giblin, p. 127 (from *The Life and Death of Adolph Hitler*).

"It is no longer . . . nationality": Robeson, p. 131 (from *Robeson Speaks*).

"I am here . . .": Robeson, quoted in Duberman, p. 228.

"It was the one . . .": Robeson, quoted in Seton, p. 121.

"nature-cure": Duberman, p. 231.

"*Deep river . . .*": from "Deep River," African-American spiritual.

"weakened or changed": Robeson, quoted in Duberman, p. 231.

"Having helped on . . .": Robeson, p. 127 (from *Robeson Speaks*).

chapter 20

"buoyant mood . . . leadership to his people": Robeson, Paul Jr., p. 332 (from *Undiscovered Robeson, 1898–1939*).

"I feel closer . . .": Robeson, p. 130 (from *Robeson Speaks*).

"anti-fascist., whether . . .": Robeson, quoted in Robeson, Paul Jr., p. 333 (from *Undiscovered Robeson, 1898–1939*).

"the communists were . . .": Robeson, Paul Jr., p. 332 (from *Undiscovered Robeson, 1898–1939*).

"going overboard . . . politically": Robeson's lawyer, quoted in Boyle & Bunie, p. 404.

"I have never . . .": Robinson, Earl, quoted in Duberman, p. 236.

"reflected his [Robeson's] . . .": Brown, quoted in Seton, p. 127.

"Man in white . . . AMERICA!": from "Ballad for Americans," Robinson, Earl and John Latouche, Victor Symphony Orchestra, Courtesy RCA Victor Records.

"making radio history": Corwin, Norman, quoted in Duberman, p. 236.

"If you and . . .": hotel manager, quoted in Seton, p. 133.

"I thought of . . .": Seton, p. 133.

"Can we get . . .": Robeson, quoted in Seton, p. 133.

"defensive war": Robeson, quoted in Lubasch, p. 105.

"brave little Finland": Robeson, Paul Jr., p. 15 (from *Undiscovered Robeson, 1939–1976*).

"If it gets . . .": Schang, Fred, quoted in Duberman, p. 239.

"To ensure that . . .": Robeson, quoted in Duberman, pp. 240–241.

"He's gonna hafta . . .": repairman, quoted in Duberman, p. 246.

"We are all . . . tour": Robeson, Eslanda, quoted in Duberman, p. 246.

"I experienced no . . . ice": Robeson, Paul Jr., quoted in Tuhus.

"I can tell . . .": Letter to Paul Robeson from Ruby Heide, CIO Servicmen's Center, 150 Golden Gate Avenue, San Francisco, Friday.

"His strategy was . . .": Robeson, Paul Jr., p. 31 (from *Undiscovered Robeson, 1939–1976*).

"the bitterest resentment . . .": Robeson, quoted in Duberman, p. 255.

"the most evil . . .": Hoover, quoted in Gentry, p. 81.

"was practically controlled . . . leanings": Hoover, quoted in Gentry, p. 207.

"agents": FBI agent, quoted in Cunningham, p. 80.

"reputedly a member . . .": FBI agent, quoted in Duberman, p. 253.

"in its membership . . .": inspector of U.S. Immigration and Naturalization Service office, quoted in Robeson, Paul Jr., p. 24 (from *Undiscovered Robeson, 1939–1976*).

"with reference to . . .": FBIHQ File 100 -12304, Section 1, Paul Robeson, Sr.

"proof . . . made . . .": Matthews, J.B., Dies Committee of House of Representatives, quoted in Duberman, p. 239.

"Confidential": quoted in Duberman, p. 654.

chapter 21

"Here's the story . . .": from "The Four Rivers," folk song.

"I believed that . . .": Webster, quoted in Seton, p. 149.

"Everyone was scared": Webster, Margaret, quoted in Duberman, p. 263.

"Robeson is going . . .": Hagen, quoted in Duberman, p. 264.

"no technique . . . protect him": Webster, quoted in Duberman, p. 264.

"Bravo!": Duberman, p. 265.

"staid old walls . . .": reporter, quoted in Duberman, p. 265.

"A great artistic achievement": reviewer, quoted in Duberman, p. 265.

"heroic and convincing": *New York Times*, quoted in Duberman, p. 265.

"No white man . . .": *Variety*, quoted in Duberman, p. 265.

"discovered that they . . .": Brown, quoted in Watterson, p. 57.

"a war for . . .": Robeson, quoted in Duberman, p. 266.

"The Communists": Duberman, p. 266.

"His activities . . .": FBI, quoted in Duberman, p. 254.

"My father was . . .": Robeson, Paul Jr., p. 55 (from *Undiscovered Robeson, 1939–1976*).

"You'll be a target . . . around you": Robeson, quoted in Robeson, Paul Jr., p. 56 (from *Undiscovered Robeson, 1939–1976*).

"I do what . . .": Robeson, quoted in Robeson, Paul Jr., p. 56 (from *Undiscovered Robeson, 1939–1976*).

"I don't have it": Robeson, quoted in Duberman, p. 269.

"Directors assumed . . .": Robeson, quoted in Duberman, p. 270.

"Just look at . . .": Webster, quoted in Duberman, p. 271.

"I took *Othello* . . .," "as a great . . .," "I am not . . .": Robeson, quoted in Seton, p. 152.

"Out of my head": Robeson, quoted in Seton, p. 152.

"constantly careful . . .": Robeson, quoted in Duberman, p. 275.

"The performance was . . .": Robeson, Paul Jr., p. 59 (from *Undiscovered Robeson, 1939–1976*).

"The family loved the . . .": Robeson, Eslanda, quoted in Robeson, Paul Jr., p. 59 (from *Undiscovered Robeson, 1939–1976*).

"I have never . . .": Webster, Margaret, quoted in Duberman, p. 276.

"I pray you . . . die upon a kiss": Shakespeare, William, pp. 152–153.

"the tormented Moor . . . final moment . . . Mary Jane shoes": Popper, April 1978.

"Paul, we are all . . .": Webster, quoted in Lubasch, p. 119.

"one of the most . . .": *World-Telegram*, quoted in Duberman, p. 277.

"Paul began to beam . . .": McGhee, Bert, quoted in Seton, p. 154.

"Boy I'm lucky . . .": Robeson, quoted in Seton, p. 154.

chapter 22

"undoubtedly 100% Communist": FBI agents, quoted in Duberman, p. 280.

"custodial detention . . . to Communism": FBI agents, quoted in Duberman, p. 254.

"activities in behalf . . .": Duberman, p. 254.

"I come here . . . toward Negroes": Robeson, pp. 151–152 (from *Robeson Speaks*).

"the tallest . . .": Bethune, quoted in Duberman, p. 285.

"Save your voice . . .": audience member, quoted in Duberman, p. 285.

"Happy birthday . . .": chorus, quoted in Duberman, p. 285.

"security index . . .": Hoover, quoted in Robeson, Paul Jr., p. 63 (from *Undiscovered Robeson, 1939–1976*).

"rights of man . . .": Robeson, quoted in Duberman, p. 294.

"inspired black . . .": Robeson, Paul Jr., p. 104 (from *Undiscovered Robeson, 1939–1976*).

"*I'se so weary* . . .": "Ol' Man River," as modified by Robeson.

"As he sang . . . .": serviceman, quoted in Robeson, Paul Jr., p. 103 (from
  Undiscovered Robeson, 1939–1976).

"to the man . . .": Lubasch, p. 123.

"uppity": Duberman, p. 305.

"Full employment . . . non-existent": Robeson, quoted in Duberman, p. 300.

"foul mood": Brown, quoted in Duberman, p. 302.

"more difficult . . . another concert": Brown, quoted in Seton, p. 169.

"*Stop the* . . . evil": Robeson, quoted in Duberman, p. 305.

"an American crusade . . ." Duberman, p. 306.

"inept . . . this country . . . threat": Lubasch, p. 126.

"People of America . . .": Lubasch, p. 128.

"of the lynch . . .": Robeson, quoted in Lubasch, p. 128.

"He is not . . . United States": Robeson, quoted in Robeson, Paul Jr., p. 112
  (from *Undiscovered Robeson, 1939–1976*).

"I ask it . . .": committee chairman, quoted in Robeson, Paul Jr., p. 113 (from
  Undiscovered Robeson, 1939–1976).

"No. I am not . . . a Communist": Robeson, quoted in Robeson, Paul Jr, p. 113
  (from *Undiscovered Robeson, 1939–1976*).

chapter 23

"*I dreamed I saw* . . .": from "Joe Hill," Music by Earl Robinson, lyrics by Alfred
  Hayes.

"You've heard . . .": Robeson, quoted in Lubasch, p. 131.

"The best way. . .": Stewart, Jeffery. *Paul Robeson: Artist and Citizen*, p. 181.

"disloyal": Giblin, p. 64 (from *The Rise and Fall of Senator Joe McCarthy*).

"remained outwardly unconcerned": Robeson, Paul Jr., p. 116 (from
  Undiscovered Robeson, 1939–1976).

"I have been . . .": Robeson, quoted in Lubasch, p. 131.

"nothing criminal in the . . .": Wallace, Henry, quoted in Duberman, p. 325.

"I had an intense . . . went": Brown, quoted in Seton, p. 190.

"For Colored Only,": quoted in Seton, p. 190.

"For God's sake . . .": Robeson, quoted in Seton, p. 190.

"I do not fear . . .": Robeson, quoted in Duberman, p. 336.

"the English public . . .": Brown, quoted in Duberman, p. 338.

"I have come among . . . Colonial Countries,": Robeson quoted in, Paul
    Robeson Jr. (from *Undiscovered Robeson, 1939–1976*), p. 142.

"on the backs . . . among all nations": Duberman, p. 342.

"dismissed and forgotten": critic, quoted in Duberman, p. 343.

"just plain screwy": *New York Amsterdam News*, quoted in Duberman, p. 343.

"act nice . . . of noise": Duberman, p. 343.

"many Negroes will be . . ." White, quoted in Duberman, p. 343.

"There is hardly . . .": North Carolina newspaper, quoted in Duberman, p. 345.

"mistaken and misled . . . Robeson": *New York Times*, quoted in Duberman,
    p. 349.

"This has been such . . .": Robeson, quoted in Duberman, p. 349.

"*I met my brother . . .*": from "Scandalize My Name," African-American spiritual.

"how deeply touched . . .": Robeson, quoted in Duberman, p. 352.

chapter 24

"This is an . . .": Robeson quoted in Richard Carter, "Robeson Home, Met by
    Cops," *Daily Compass*, June 17, 1949.

"documents of interest": Goodman, p. 84.

"screaming all . . .": Greenberg, quoted in Duberman, p. 355.

"outraged . . . Soviet Union": Robeson, quoted in Paul Robeson Jr. (from
    Undiscovered Robeson, 1939–1976) p. 359.

"I have the . . .": Robeson, Susan, p. 165 (from *The Whole World In His Hands:
    A Pictorial Biography of Paul Robeson*).

"Hello there . . . hard": Robeson, quoted in Robeson, Paul Jr., p. 160 (from
    Undiscovered Robeson, 1939–1976).

"I fight for the right . . .": *Robeson Speaks*, p. 202.

"They want peace . . . WILL NOT": *Robeson Speaks*, p. 209.

"We do not want . . . human beings": *Robeson Speaks*, p. 211.

"Loves Soviet . . .": Duberman, p. 358.

"It was an accident . . .": Duberman, p. 358.

"silly . . . personal views": Robinson, quoted in Duberman, p. 360.

"no argument between . . .": Robeson, quoted in Duberman, p. 362.

"un-American": Peekskill Junior Chamber of Commerce, quoted in
    Duberman, p. 364.

"Dirty Commie" and "Dirty kike": crowd members, quoted in Duberman, p. 365.

"hardened to threats": Seton, p. 207.

"Get the . . .": Rosen, Helen, quoted in Duberman, p. 365.

"Wake Up . . .": Duberman, p. 368.

"We'll kill . . .": crowd, quoted in Turell (video).

"I came here . . .": Robeson, quoted in Robeson, Paul Jr., p. 172 (from *Undiscovered Robeson, 1939–1976*).

"as big as . . . attack": Seeger, quoted in Lubasch, p. 154.

"watched in silent horror": Robeson, Paul Jr., p. 175 (from *Undiscovered Robeson, 1939–1976*).

"the police who . . . yesterday": Robeson, quoted in Duberman, p. 370.

"If anyone I . . .": Robeson, Eslanda, quoted in Duberman, p. 374.

"battle of Peekskill": Duberman, p. 372.

"lawlessness . . . from doing so": Roosevelt, Eleanor, quoted in Robeson, Paul Jr., p. 177 (from *Undiscovered Robeson, 1939–1976*).

"I shall tak. . . . prevail": Robeson, quoted in Seton, p. 215.

chapter 25

"I'll also be . . ." Robeson, quoted in Duberman, p. 375.

"There is a balm . . .": from "Balm in Gilead," African-American spiritual.

"an invasion": Los Angeles City Council, quoted in Duberman, p. 376.

"indiscriminate character assassination": *New York Times*, quoted in Giblin, p. 88 (from *The Rise and Fall of Senator Joe McCarthy*).

"the Negro . . .": Duberman, p. 384.

"decent Americans": American Legion and Catholic War Veterans, quoted in Duberman, p. 384.

"the final say . . .": Roosevelt, Eleanor, quoted in Lubasch, p. 157.

"a sad commentary . . .": Robeson, quoted in Duberman, p. 385.

"deeply hurt . . .": Seton, p. 222.

"The basic . . .": Robeson, quoted in Lubasch, p. 158.

"What is the . . .," "Jim-Crow Justice! . . .,": Robeson, quoted in Duberman, p. 387.

Our enemies . . .": Robeson, quoted in Duberman, p. 387

"The place for . . .": Robeson, quoted in Robeson, Paul Jr., p. 212 (from *Undiscovered Robeson, 1939–1976*).

"was fully . . .": Seton, p. 223.

"stop notice," Duberman, p. 388.

"FBI agents intruded . . . ": Robeson, Paul Jr., p. 212 (from *Undiscovered Robeson, 1939–1976*).

"The Department considers . . . detrimental . . . family affair": U.S. State Department, quoted in Duberman, p. 389.

"to silence . . .": Robeson, quoted in Duberman, p. 390.

chapter 26

"Paul, were you . . . American": Robeson, p. 259 (from *Robeson Speaks*).

"slave origin": Robeson, p. 260 (from *Robeson Speaks*).

"I refuse to . . .": Robeson, p. 260 (from *Robeson Speaks*).

"I just wanted . . .": Parker, quoted in Lubasch, p. 161.

"a sort of . . .": Robeson, quoted in Duberman, pp. 399–400.

"across-the-border": Murphy, Harvey, quoted in Duberman, p. 400.

"I can't tell . . .": Robeson, quoted in Lubasch, p. 162.

"comes from the . . .": Robeson, quoted in Lubasch, p. 163.

"*No more driver's . . .*": from "No More Auction Block for Me," African-American spiritual.

"What would my . . .": Robeson, quoted in Lubasch, p. 163.

"Paul felt safe . . .": Robeson, Paul Jr., p. 229 (from *Undiscovered Robeson, 1939–1976*).

"the struggle against war": Lubasch, p. 164.

"in the name of . . .": Robeson, quoted in Robeson, Paul Jr., p. 227 (from *Undiscovered Robeson, 1939–1976*).

"You are Mrs. Paul . . .": committee member, quoted in Lubasch, p. 164.

"Yes, and very proud . . .": Robeson, Eslanda, quoted in Lubasch, p. 164.

"I don't quite . . ." Robeson, Eslanda, quoted in Lubasch, p. 164.

"good chance . . . United States": committee member, quoted in Lubasch, p. 164.

"The reason I refuse . . .": Robeson, Eslanda, quoted in Lubasch, p. 165.

"Why don't you ask him": Robeson, Eslanda, quoted in Robeson, Paul Jr.,
    p. 228 (from *Undiscovered Robeson, 1939–1976*).

"soldiers of the fight": liner notes by Paul Robeson Jr., 2006 interview quoted
    in "On My Journey Now: Paul Robeson's Independent Recordings," #5.
    "We are Climbing Jacob's Ladder," Alan Booth, piano, Carnegie Recital
    Hall, 1955, p. 25.

"Salute to Paul Robeson": Duberman, p. 425.

"Let Robeson Sing": Duberman, p. 424-425.

"the stirrings of . . .": Robeson, quoted in Duberman, p. 431.

"magnificent stride forward": Robeson, quoted in Duberman, p. 430.

"fight to see . . .": Robeson, quoted in Duberman, p. 431.

"heroic": Robeson, quoted in Duberman, p. 430.

"forerunner . . . participant": Robeson, Paul Jr., p. 245 (from *Undiscovered
    Robeson, 1939–1976*).

"one of the most . . .": government attorney, quoted in Duberman, p. 433.

"a prisoner in his . . .": Robeson, quoted in Duberman, p. 435.

"Suddenly everything changed": Robeson, Paul Jr., p. 249 (from *Undiscovered
    Robeson, 1939–1976*).

chapter 27

"slumped in his chair . . .": Robeson, Paul Jr., p. 249 (from *Undiscovered Robeson,
    1939–1976*).

"going haywire": Duberman, p. 440.

"he sat bolt . . . outset": Robeson, Paul Jr., p. 249 (from *Undiscovered Robeson,
    1939–1976*).

"Are you now . . .": Arens, quoted in Robeson, Paul Jr., p. 250 (from
    Undiscovered Robeson, 1939–1976).

"Oh please . . .": quoted in Robeson, Paul Jr., p. 250 (from *Undiscovered Robeson,
    1939–1976*).

"What do you mean . . . over the world": Robeson, quoted in Robeson, Paul
    Jr., p. 250 (from *Undiscovered Robeson, 1939–1976*).

"I put it to you": Arens, quoted in Robeson, Paul Jr., p. 250 (from *Undiscovered
    Robeson, 1939–1976*).

"I invoke . . . ridiculous": Robeson, quoted in Robeson, Paul Jr., p. 250 (from *Undiscovered Robeson, 1939–1976*).

"I am not being . . .": Robeson, quoted in Robeson, Paul Jr., p. 251 (from *Undiscovered Robeson, 1939–1976*).

"In Russia I . . . committee today": Robeson, quoted in Robeson, Paul Jr., p. 252–253 (from *Undiscovered Robeson, 1939–1976*).

"Why do you not . . .": Scherer, quoted in Robeson, Paul Jr., p. 253 (from *Undiscovered Robeson, 1939–1976*).

"Because my father . . . that clear?": Robeson, quoted in Robeson, Paul Jr., p. 253 (from *Undiscovered Robeson, 1939–1976*).

"to spare him . . .": Duberman, p. 441.

"What prejudice . . . Rutgers": Walter, Francis, quoted in Duberman. p. 441.

"the success of . . .": Robeson, quoted in Duberman. p. 441.

"un-Americans . . . this forever . . . standing my ground": Robeson, quoted in Duberman, p. 442.

"Mr. Robeson is . . .": *Afro-American*, quoted in Robeson, Paul Jr., p. 254 (from *Undiscovered Robeson, 1939–1976*).

"I hope to . . .": Batten, Tony, executive producer. *A Profile of Paul Robeson*. Greater Washington Educational Telecommunications Association, 1975.

"I am sorry . . .": Robeson, quoted in Duberman, p. 454.

"the years have . . .": critic, quoted in Duberman, p. 455.

"nervous as . . . voice": Robeson, Eslanda, quoted in Duberman, p. 460.

"because he has . . .": Nehru, quoted in Duberman, p. 461.

"Join me": Robeson, *Paul Robeson Live at Carnegie Hall: The Historic May 9, 1958 Concert*. Vanguard Records, 1987.

"*We are climbing . . .*": from "Jacob's Ladder," African-American spiritual.

"lost much . . . charm": critics, quoted in Duberman, p. 462.

"I want the folks . . .": Robeson, quoted in Duberman, p. 463.

"A wonderful thing . . ." Robeson quoted by reporters, *London-Newark News*, July 11, 1958.

"a victory for . . .": Robeson, quoted in Duberman, p. 463.

"and, of course . . .": Robeson, quoted in Anderson, David, no page given.

"The long years . . .": Robeson, Eslanda, quoted in Lubasch, p. 185.

"I've been a part . . .": Robeson, quoted in Duberman, p. 522.

"While I must . . .": Robeson, quoted in Lubasch, p. 189.

"We of . . .": speaker, quoted in Lubasch, p. 191.

"Goodbye, Paul!": *Amsterdam News*, quoted in Lubasch, p. 203.

"The tallest tree . . .": Brown, quoted in Lubasch, p. 204.

"the artist must elect . . ." Lubasch, p. 204.

"There is more . . .": Robeson, p. 473 (from *Robeson Speaks*).

"Didn't my Lord . . .": "Didn't My Lord Deliver Daniel," African-American spiritual.

index

Page numbers in **boldface** refer to images and/or captions.

Washington, DC, 35, 168, 184,
185, 199, 209, 217, 218, **219**,
220

Webster, Margaret, 172, 174, 176,
177, 178

Wells, H. G., 118

Welsh Miners' Relief Fund, 100

Westchester Committee for Law
and Order, 200

Westfield, New Jersey, 31, 33

White, Walter, 70, 80–81, 193

Wilcoxon, Henry, **145**, 146

Wilkins, Roy, 92

Williams, Bert, 91

Wilmington, Delaware, 89

Wilson, Woodrow, 27

Winants Hall, 38–39, 44

Witherspoon Street, **26**, 27, 30,
228

Witherspoon School for
Colored Children, 28, **29**,
37

Witherspoon Street
Presbyterian Church, 25, 27

Woollcott, Alexander, 58, 68, 90

working class, 64, 115, 137, 138,
144, 146, 157, 207

World Congress of Partisans of
Peace, 191, **192**, 198

World Peace Council (WPC), 206

World-Telegram, 178

World War I, 38, 46, 65, 145

World War II, 154–155, 156, 161,
166, 181, **182**, 197, 198

Y

YMCA, **29**, 44, 170

Z

Ziegfeld, Florenz, 90, 91, 92, 93

song index

picture credits

Alamy Stock Photo, dpa picture alliance: 128 (bottom); SPUTNIK/ Alamy Stock Photo: 132; Lebrecht Music and Arts Photo Library/ Alamy Stock Photo: 149 (top); ZUMA Press., Inc.: 154-155.

Billy Rose Theatre Division, New York Public Library for the Performing Arts, Astor, Lenox and Tilden Foundations: 18.

Carl Van Vechten, and © Van Vechten Trust: 20 (bottom), 60 (top), 140 (bottom).

Courtesy Beinecke Rare Book & Manuscript Collection, Yale University: 16.

Doris Ulmann, photographer. Courtesy of Peter Fetterman: 8.

FBI—Paul Robeson, Sr., Part 1 of 31, Government Publication— Bibliography/Chicago Style Guide/Citefast: 169.

Getty Images: 112 (top), 119, 120, 128 (top), 140 (top), 151, 163, 182 (bottom), 189 (top and bottom), 192 (bottom), 202, 203 (top), 207, 216 (top), 219, 225 (top and bottom).

Historical Society of Princeton: 26 (bottom), 29 (bottom).

Lebrecht Music & Arts Photo Library: 82 (top).

Library of Congress, Prints and Photographs Division: LC-USZ62-123429, 100; LC-USZ62-91536, 112 (bottom); LC-USZ62-127379, 134; LC-H22-D-8745, 167; LC-USZ62-39852, 182 (top); LC-USZ62-119697, 192 (top); LOC Control # 2011645172, NYWTS-SUB-GEOG-Riots-NY, 203 (bottom); LOC Control #95512127, Call NYWTS-BIOG-McCarthy J, 205; Photo ID: 083.00.00, 216 (bottom).

text and song permissions

Alfred Publishing, LLC, *Ballad for Americans*: 163, 164.

Copyright Clearance Center on behalf of Hachette Books Group. *The Young Paul Robeson: On my journey now*: 31, 33, 35, 37, 39, 41, 43, 44, 48, 51, 53, 64, 66, 129.

Hal Leonard LLC, *Ol' Man River*: 95, 150, 183; *Joe Hill*: 187, *Ballad for Americans*: 163, 164.

"Let the Rail Splitter Awake and Other Poems" by Pablo Neruda. Copyright © 1970, 1988 by International Publishers. Reprinted with Permission, all rights reserved: 5.

Copyright © 1989 Martin Duberman from *Paul Robeson: A Biography* reprinted by permission of The Frances Goldin Literary Agency: 14, 17, 21, 22, 23, 25, 27, 30, 34, 35, 37, 39, 43, 44, 45, 46, 47, 48, 50, 53, 55, 56, 57, 58, 61, 62, 64, 65, 67, 69, 70, 71, 73, 74, 75, 76, 77, 79, 80, 81, 86, 89, 92, 94, 95, 97, 98, 99, 102, 104, 105, 106, 107, 108, 109, 110, 111, 115, 116, 117, 118, 123, 124, 125, 126, 136, 137, 138, 139, 142, 143, 144, 145, 146, 148, 150, 153, 156, 157, 160, 161, 163, 164, 165, 166, 168, 170, 172, 174, 175, 176, 177, 178, 179, 180, 181, 183, 184, 188, 191, 193, 194, 196, 198, 199, 200, 201, 202, 204, 206, 207, 208, 209, 211, 215, 217, 219, 220, 221, 222, 223, 224.

Robeson: An American Ballad by Arnold Lubasch Copyright © 2012. Used by permission of Rowman & Littlefield Publishing Group. All Rights Reserved: 22, 73, 77, 80, 81, 83, 85, 92, 93,101, 106, 114, 118, 123, 129, 138, 142, 143, 144, 146, 147, 148, 150, 152, 156, 165, 178, 183, 185, 187, 188, 201, 206, 211, 212, 213, 214, 224, 226, 227, 228.

Robeson Family Trust: *The Whole World In His Hands* by Susan Robeson: 165; *Here I Stand* by Paul Robeson: 13, 24, 28, 31, 32, 33, 35, 36, 38, 62, 65, 95; *Paul Robeson Speaks*, edited by Phil Foner: 13, 17, 27, 85, 97, 103, 126, 131, 133, 135, 137, 138, 143, 145, 147, 158, 161, 162, 198,

Award-winning nonfiction author

Susan Goldman Rubin

met Paul Robeson when she was a teenager
growing up in the Bronx. Susan is the author of
more than 55 books for young people, including
*Coco Chanel: Pearls, Perfume, and the Little Black
Dress; Music Was It! Young Leonard Bernstein;*
and *Freedom Summer: The 1964 Struggle for
Civil Rights in Mississippi.* She lives in Malibu,
California. Visit her at susangoldmanrubin.com.